In the

Prophet's Garden

A selection of ahadith for the young

Compiled by

Fatima M D'Oyen *and* Abdelkader Chachi

THE ISLAMIC FOUNDATION

Published by

THE ISLAMIC FOUNDATION

Markfield Conference Centre
Ratby Lane, Markfield
Leicester LE67 9SY, United Kingdom
E-mail: publications@islamic-foundation.com
Website: www.islamic-foundation.com

Quran House, P.O. Box 30611, Nairobi, Kenya

P.M.B. 3193, Kano, Nigeria

Distributed by
Kube Publishing Ltd.
Tel: +44(01530) 249230, Fax: +44(01530) 249656
E-mail: info@kubepublishing.com

British Library Cataloguing-in-Publication Data
D'Oyen, Fatima M.; In the Prophet's Garden:
a selection of ahadith for the young
1. Hadith - Juvenile literature. Ummah (Islam)
I. Title II. Chachi, Abdelkader
III. Islamic Foundation
297. 1'24

ISBN 978 0 86037 372 X

Cover/Book design & typeset: Nasir Cadir

Notes

This book uses the name 'Allah' throughout
when referring to the One Eternal God,
Lord and Creator of the Universe,
Glorified is He!

Allah is the proper name of God for all native
Arabic-speakers, regardless of religion,
and it is the name Muslims prefer to use for God.

In conformity with Islamic tradition, the following calligraphic symbols
have been used to indicate respect:

ﷺ = (peace and blessings be upon him) when mentioning Prophet
    Muhammad,

ﷵ = (on him be peace) when mentioning any other Prophet,

ﵿ = (May Allah be pleased with him) for the Prophet's Companions.

ﵿ = (May Allah be pleased with her) for the Prophet's Companions.

Contents

Preface

All thanks and praise is due to Allah Most High, who guides whomever He wills to the path of eternal happiness through the wonderful example of His beloved Prophet Muhammad ﷺ whom He entrusted with His Message.

Many worthy collections of hadith (plural ahadith: sayings and deeds) of the Prophet Muhammad ﷺ have been compiled and translated into English. Very few, however, have been compiled specifically for children and young people, and this collection is intended to fill that gap. In the Prophet's Garden presents two hundred authentic ahadith that will appeal to all ages but are especially suitable for young people, taking into consideration their vocabulary, needs and interests. We have therefore selected ahadith that are fairly self-explanatory, and have kept notes to a bare minimum. Where only part of a hadith relates to the chapter topic only the relevant part has been included; also, the name of the narrator has not been given except when needed for clarification (although the authority for each hadith is named, e.g. Bukhari). The selected ahadith have been taken from a wide range of authentic sources: the collections of Imams Bukhari, Muslim, Abu Dawud, Tirmidhi, Nasa'i, Ibn Majah, Bayhaqi, Malik and al-Darimi.

While we have remained close to the literal meaning of the original texts, some Arabic expressions have been paraphrased to make them easier to understand. The Arabic texts are included for ease of reference, although we assume that anyone who wishes to study them in-depth or memorise them will do so under the guidance of a scholar. Finally, transliteration marks have not been used for Arabic letters except to represent ʿayn (ʿ) and hamza ('), in order to keep things simple.

This small book has been the collaborative effort of many. We would like to extend our sincere gratitude to Dr. Manazir Ahsan and Dr. Muhammad Isa Waley for their help with revising the translations, seeking alternative ahadith, and offering their encouragement and support, and to Dr. A. R. Kidwai and Sarah Nakhoodah for their helpful editorial suggestions. We would also like to thank brothers Anwar Cara and Nasir Cadir for the lovely layout and design.

It is our hope that 'In the Prophet's Garden' will serve as a useful introduction to the timeless wisdom of the last Prophet of Islam ﷺ both at home and in the classroom, and we pray that on the Last Day it will atone for some of our sins. We ask our Lord's forgiveness and readers' indulgence for any faults or omissions, welcome any suggestions for improvement.

Rabi' al-Thani 1423 H
June 2002

Fatima M D'Oyen
Abdelkader Chachi

Introduction

In the name of Allah, the Most Compassionate, the Most Merciful

What is a *Hadith*?

In the Arabic language the word hadith (plural ahadith, or hadiths) means 'news'; it also means 'saying, report, speech or story'. In the context of Islam, when we speak of hadith we mean the Prophet Muhammad's ﷺ sayings, deeds, advice, and the actions approved in his presence, as recorded by his Companions. Ahadith are sometimes referred to as Traditions. A related word is Sunnah, which means 'way of life.' It is used to mean the Way of the Prophet ﷺ. We learn about his Sunnah from ahadith, as well as from the customs and rulings of his pious Companions, who modelled their lives after his.

Why are *Ahadith* important?

After the Qur'an itself – God's Last Testament and revelation to mankind – the Sunnah is the second source of Islam. The Qur'an lays down basic principles, while the Sunnah clarifies those principles and explains how to put them into practice. For instance, Allah states in the Qur'an that Muslims must pray, give charity, fast and make pilgrimage, but the details of how to fulfil those essential obligations were taught by the Prophet Muhammad ﷺ. It would be impossible to practise Islam correctly without knowledge of the Prophet's Sunnah. The importance of the Prophet's role as a teacher, advisor and lawgiver is emphasised in the Qur'an in many verses. Allah says:

Whatever the Messenger (of Allah) gives you, take it;
and whatever he forbids, avoid. (al-Qur'an 59: 7)

Obey Allah and the Messenger... (al-Qur'an 3:132)

He does not speak from his own desire (al-Qur'an 53:3)

How do we know what the Prophet Muhammad ﷺ said and did?
The Prophet's Companions were utterly devoted to him, and out of their
love for him they tried to emulate his way of doing things, and to remember
his every word. They also knew that Allah would hold them responsible for
passing on the Prophet's teachings to the next generation of Muslims.
The Prophet ﷺ instructed them, 'Pass on knowledge from me, even if it is
only one sentence,' and 'those who are present should convey the message
to those who are absent' (Bukhari). He made this easier for them by speaking
in short sentences and sometimes repeating important points three times.
Those Companions who had good memories would spend some time each
day repeating what they had heard from Allah's Messenger; some formed
study circles for this purpose or wrote down his teachings in books for their
personal reference. Abu Hurayrah ﷺ, who transmitted thousands of ahadith,
used to divide his night into three parts: one third for sleeping, one third for
praying, and one third for memorising ahadith. Other Companions including
ʿUmar, ʿAli, Abu Musa al-Ashʿari, Ibn Masʿud, Ibn ʿAbbas, and ʿA'ishah
also devoted much time to memorising the Prophet's words and teaching
them to others (may Allah be pleased with them all). They were extremely
cautious not to make mistakes, because of the Prophet's ﷺ warning: 'Whoever
deliberately tells a lie about me will find his place ready in Hellfire' (Tirmidhi).

How the teaching of *Hadith* spread
After the Prophet's ﷺ death, his Companions and their Successors continued
to teach the Qur'an and hadith at mosques and study circles. Students

everywhere, from India, China, and Afghanistan to Egypt, North Africa and Spain devoted themselves to memorising the Prophet's words and following his blessed example. Scholars travelled from city to city to learn or to teach, quoting the sources of each hadith they knew. A scholar might say, 'I heard from Ibn Wahb, who heard from 'Amr, who heard from Bukhayr, who heard from Ibn al-Musayyab, who heard from Abu Hurayrah, that the blessed Prophet ﷺ said...' and he would narrate the hadith. The chain of narrators became known as the sanad, while the hadith itself was known as the matn, or text.

How the sciences of *hadith* were established

As Islam spread far and wide, and many different kinds of people had dealings with Muslims, it became increasingly difficult to be sure that all the things being said in the Prophet's ﷺ name were, in fact, true. Some hypocrites and enemies of Islam began to invent and to spread false ahadith, to try to get support for their own ideas and opinions. When this happened, scholars developed a scientific method for how to sort true ahadith from false ones. In order for a matn to be authentic it had to fulfil certain conditions; for instance, it must not contradict the Qur'an, must make sense, and must be in correct Arabic. An accurate way of investigating the sanad was also developed, and any hadith whose narrators were not totally trustworthy, pious Muslims with good memories was rejected. Scholars specialising in ahadith compiled their authentic collections into books, which have been used ever since. The most famous and authentic of these are the collections of Imams Bukhari, Muslim, Nasa'i, Abu Dawud, Tirmidhi, and Ibn Majah (known as al-Sihah al-Sittah, or the six authentic collections), along with the Muwatta' of Imam Malik. Most ahadith can be found in two or more of these collections; those which have been recorded by both Bukhari and Muslim are known as mutaffaqun 'alayh (agreed upon), and are considered especially reliable.

Learning _Hadith_ today

Muslims have continued the tradition of memorising ahadith as well as the Qur'an in Arabic up to the present day. Although one can learn about the teachings of the Prophet Muhammad ﷺ through reading books, if one makes the effort to memorise hadith under the guidance of a teacher it has a stronger effect on the heart. It also helps to improve one's knowledge of Arabic. A person who learns hadith in this way is more likely to remember the Prophet's ﷺ teachings, and be inspired to act on them. All Muslims, young and old, are encouraged to memorise at least forty ahadith in Arabic because, as the Prophet ﷺ said: 'Whoever memorises and preserves forty ahadith for my people relating to their religion, Allah will resurrect him among the scholars and martyrs on the Last Day.' May Allah help us to attain this worthy goal. Success is through Him alone.

1

Who was the Prophet Muhammad ﷺ, and what was he like?

كَمَآ أَرْسَلْنَا فِيكُمْ رَسُولًا مِّنكُمْ يَتْلُواْ عَلَيْكُمْ ءَايَٰتِنَا وَيُزَكِّيكُمْ وَيُعَلِّمُكُمُ ٱلْكِتَٰبَ وَٱلْحِكْمَةَ وَيُعَلِّمُكُم مَّا لَمْ تَكُونُواْ تَعْلَمُونَ ﴿١٥١﴾

We have sent you a Messenger of your own who recites
Our revelations to you and makes you grow in purity;
and educates you in the Scripture, and wisdom,
and teaches you what you knew nothing about. (al-Qur'an 2:151)

قُلْ إِنَّمَآ أَنَا۠ بَشَرٌ مِّثْلُكُمْ يُوحَىٰٓ إِلَىَّ أَنَّمَآ إِلَٰهُكُمْ إِلَٰهٌ وَٰحِدٌ فَمَن كَانَ يَرْجُواْ لِقَآءَ رَبِّهِۦ فَلْيَعْمَلْ عَمَلًا صَٰلِحًا وَلَا يُشْرِكْ بِعِبَادَةِ رَبِّهِۦٓ أَحَدَۢا ﴿١١٠﴾

'Say (O Muhammad): I am only human, like yourselves.
It is revealed to me that your god is (only) One God.
So whoever hopes to meet his Lord should do good deeds,
and not worship anyone but his Lord.' (al-Qur'an 18:110)

I

قَالَ رَسُولُ اللّهِ صَلَّى اللّهُ عَلَيْهِ وَسَلَّمَ: إِنَّ مَثَلِي وَمَثَلَ الأَنْبِيَاءِ مِنْ قَبْلِي كَمَثَلِ رَجُلٍ بَنَى بَيْتًا فَأَحْسَنَهُ وَأَجْمَلَهُ إِلاَّ مَوْضِعَ لَبِنَةٍ مِنْ زَاوِيَةٍ فَجَعَلَ النَّاسُ يَطُوفُونَ بِهِ وَيَعْجَبُونَ لَهُ وَيَقُولُونَ هَلاَّ وُضِعَتْ هَذِهِ اللَّبِنَةُ، قَالَ: فَأَنَا اللَّبِنَةُ وَأَنَا خَاتِمُ النَّبِيِّينَ. (البخاري)

THE PROPHET ﷺ said: 'My likeness in relation to the Prophets who came before me is that of a man who built a house, and made it fine and lovely, except that one brick in its corner was missing. The people went around it and wondered at its beauty, but said: 'If only that brick were put in its place!' I am that brick, and I am the seal of the Prophets'. (*Bukhari*)

2

قَالَ رَسُولُ اللّهِ صَلَّى اللّهُ عَلَيْهِ وَسَلَّمَ: كَانَ النَّبِيُّ يُبْعَثُ إِلَى قَوْمِهِ خَاصَّةً، وَبُعِثْتُ إِلَى النَّاسِ عَامَّةً. (البخاري)

THE PROPHET ﷺ said: 'Every Prophet before me was sent to his people alone, but I have been sent to all mankind'. (Bukhari)

3

كَانَ عَلِيٌّ رَضِيَ اللَّهُ عَنْهُ إِذَا وَصَفَ النَّبِيَّ صَلَّى اللَّهُ عَلَيْهِ وَسَلَّمَ قَالَ: مَنْ رَآهُ بَدِيهَةً هَابَهُ، وَمَنْ خَالَطَهُ مَعْرِفَةً أَحَبَّهُ، يَقُولُ نَاعِتُهُ: لَمْ أَرَ قَبْلَهُ وَلَا بَعْدَهُ مِثْلَهُ. (الترمذي)

'ALI ibn Abi Talib ﷺ (describing the Prophet ﷺ) said: 'Anyone who saw him suddenly would stand in awe of him, and anyone who got to know him through spending time with him came to love him. Those who described him said that they had never seen anyone like him, before or since'. (*Tirmidhi*)

4

عَنْ أَنَسِ بْنِ مَالِكٍ رَضِيَ اللَّهُ عَنْهُ قَالَ: خَدَمْتُ النَّبِيَّ صَلَّى اللَّهُ عَلَيْهِ وَسَلَّمَ عَشْرَ سِنِينَ فَمَا قَالَ لِي أُفٍّ قَطُّ، وَمَا قَالَ لِشَيْءٍ صَنَعْتُهُ لِمَ صَنَعْتَهُ، وَلَا لِشَيْءٍ تَرَكْتُهُ لِمَ تَرَكْتَهُ، وَكَانَ رَسُولُ اللَّهِ صَلَّى اللَّهُ عَلَيْهِ وَسَلَّمَ مِنْ أَحْسَنِ النَّاسِ خُلُقًا. (الترمذي)

ANAS ibn Malik ﷺ said: 'I was in the Prophet's ﷺ service for ten years, and he never once said "Uff (i.e. shame)!" to me. When I did something (wrong) he never asked me, "Why did you do that?" When I did not do something (that I should have done) he never asked me, "Why did you not do that?" The Messenger of Allah ﷺ had the best disposition of all people'. (*Tirmidhi*)

5

عَنْ عَبْدِ اللهِ بْنِ جَعْفَرٍ رَضِيَ اللهُ عَنْهُ قَالَ: كَانَ رَسُولُ اللهِ صَلَّى اللهُ عَلَيْهِ وَسَلَّمَ إِذَا قَدِمَ مِنْ سَفَرٍ
تُلُقِّيَ بِصِبْيَانِ أَهْلِ بَيْتِهِ، قَالَ وَإِنَّهُ قَدِمَ مِنْ سَفَرٍ فَسُبِقَ بِي إِلَيْهِ فَحَمَلَنِي بَيْنَ يَدَيْهِ ثُمَّ جِيءَ بِأَحَدِ ابْنَيْ
فَاطِمَةَ فَأَرْدَفَهُ خَلْفَهُ قَالَ فَأُدْخِلْنَا الْمَدِينَةَ ثَلاثَةً عَلَى دَابَّةٍ. (مسلم)

ʿABDULLAH ibn Jaʿfar ﷺ said: 'Whenever Allah's Messenger ﷺ came
back from a journey, the children of his family used to (run to)
welcome him. This was how he once came back from a journey when
I was the first to go to him: he mounted me (on his camel) in front
of him. Then one of his daughter Fatimah's two sons came, and he
mounted him behind him, and that is how the three of us were brought
into Madinah on a single mount'. (*Muslim*)

6

عَنْ كَعْبِ بْنِ مَالِكٍ رَضِيَ اللهُ عَنْهُ قَالَ: كَانَ رَسُولُ اللهِ صَلَّى اللهُ عَلَيْهِ وَسَلَّمَ إِذَا سُرَّ اسْتَنَارَ وَجْهُهُ
حَتَّى كَأَنَّهُ قِطْعَةُ قَمَرٍ وَكُنَّا نَعْرِفُ ذَلِكَ مِنْهُ. (البخاري وأحمد)

KAʿB ibn Malik ﷺ reported: 'When the Messenger of Allah ﷺ was
pleased, his face lit up as if it was a piece of the moon. That is how we
could tell when he was pleased'. (*Bukhari, Ahmad*)

7

عَنْ عَبْدِ اللَّهِ بْنِ الْحَارِثِ رَضِيَ اللَّهُ عَنْهُ قَالَ: مَا رَأَيْتُ أَحَدًا أَكْثَرَ تَبَسُّمًا مِنْ رَسُولِ اللَّهِ صَلَّى اللَّهُ عَلَيْهِ وَسَلَّمَ. (الترمذي)

ᶜABDULLAH ibn al-Harith ﷺ said: 'I never saw anyone who smiled more than Allah's Messenger ﷺ'. (*Tirmidi*)

8

عَنْ عَائِشَةَ رَضِيَ اللَّهُ عَنْهَا قَالَتْ: كَانَ كَلَامُ رَسُولِ اللَّهِ صَلَّى اللَّهُ عَلَيْهِ وَسَلَّمَ كَلَامًا فَصْلاً، يَفْهَمُهُ كُلُّ مَنْ سَمِعَهُ. (أبو داود)

ᶜA'ISHAH ﷺ said: 'The Prophet ﷺ spoke in a simple and clear way so that all those who heard him, understood him'. (*Abu Dawud*)

9

عَنْ عَائِشَةَ رَضِيَ اللَّهُ عَنْهَا قَالَتْ: مَا ضَرَبَ رَسُولُ اللَّهِ صَلَّى اللَّهُ عَلَيْهِ وَسَلَّمَ شَيْئًا قَطُّ بِيَدِهِ، وَلاَ امْرَأَةً وَلاَ خَادِمًا إِلاَّ أَنْ يُجَاهِدَ فِي سَبِيلِ اللَّهِ. (مسلم)

ᶜA'ISHAH ﷺ said: 'The Prophet ﷺ never hit anything or anyone – not a woman or a slave – except when he was fighting in the cause of Allah'. (*Muslim*)

10

عَنْ عَائِشَةَ رَضِيَ اللَّهُ عَنْهَا قَالَتْ: مَا خُيِّرَ رَسُولُ اللَّهِ صَلَّى اللَّهُ عَلَيْهِ وَسَلَّمَ بَيْنَ أَمْرَيْنِ قَطُّ، إِلاَّ اخْتَارَ أَيْسَرَهُمَا إِلاَّ أَنْ يَكُونَ فِيهِ إِثْمٌ، فَإِنْ كَانَ إِثْمًا كَانَ أَبْعَدَ النَّاسِ مِنْهُ. (البخاري ومسلم)

'A'ISHAH ﷺ related: 'Whenever the Prophet ﷺ was given a choice (between two things) he chose whatever was easier – unless it was sinful, in which case he was more careful than anyone to avoid it'. (*Bukhari, Muslim*)

11

عَنْ جَابِرٍ رَضِيَ اللَّهُ عَنْهُ قَالَ: مَا سُئِلَ النَّبِيُّ صَلَّى اللَّهُ عَلَيْهِ وَسَلَّمَ عَنْ شَيْءٍ قَطُّ فَقَالَ لاَ. (البخاري)

JABIR ﷺ said: 'Allah's Messenger ﷺ never said no when anyone asked him for anything at all'. (*Bukhari*)

12

قَالَ رَسُولُ اللَّهِ صَلَّى اللَّهُ عَلَيْهِ وَسَلَّمَ: لاَ يُؤْمِنُ أَحَدُكُمْ حَتَّى أَكُونَ أَحَبَّ إِلَيْهِ مِنْ وَالِدِهِ وَوَلَدِهِ وَالنَّاسِ أَجْمَعِينَ. (البخاري ومسلم)

THE PROPHET ﷺ said: 'None of you (truly) believes until I am dearer to him than his own parents, his children and all mankind'. (*Bukhari, Muslim*)

13

قَالَ رَسُولُ اللّٰهِ صَلَّى اللّٰهُ عَلَيْهِ وَسَلَّمَ: مَنْ صَلَّى عَلَيَّ وَاحِدَةً صَلَّى اللّٰهُ عَلَيْهِ عَشْرًا. (مسلم)

THE PROPHET ﷺ said: 'Whoever asks Allah to bless me once will be blessed by Allah ten times over'. (*Muslim*)

14

قَالَ رَسُولُ اللّٰهِ صَلَّى اللّٰهُ عَلَيْهِ وَسَلَّمَ: مَنْ أَحَبَّ سُنَّتِي فَقَدْ أَحَبَّنِي وَمَنْ أَحَبَّنِي كَانَ مَعِي فِي الْجَنَّةِ. (الترمذي)

THE PROPHET ﷺ said: 'Whoever loves my way of life (Sunnah) loves me, and whoever loves me will be with me in Paradise'. (*Tirmidhi*)

2

What is Islam?

قُولُوٓاْ ءَامَنَّا بِٱللَّهِ وَمَآ أُنزِلَ إِلَيْنَا وَمَآ أُنزِلَ إِلَىٰٓ إِبْرَٰهِـۧمَ وَإِسْمَٰعِيلَ وَإِسْحَٰقَ

وَيَعْقُوبَ وَٱلْأَسْبَاطِ وَمَآ أُوتِيَ مُوسَىٰ وَعِيسَىٰ وَمَآ أُوتِيَ ٱلنَّبِيُّونَ

مِن رَّبِّهِمْ لَا نُفَرِّقُ بَيْنَ أَحَدٍ مِّنْهُمْ وَنَحْنُ لَهُۥ مُسْلِمُونَ ﴿١٣٦﴾

Say, 'We believe in Allah and in what was revealed to us,
and in what was revealed to Abraham, Ishmael, Isaac,
Jacob and the tribes; and in what was given to Moses and Jesus and (all)
the Prophets from their Lord. We make no distinction between any of them,
and we have surrendered to Him (in Islam).' (al-Qur'an 2:136)

ٱلْيَوْمَ أَكْمَلْتُ لَكُمْ دِينَكُمْ وَأَتْمَمْتُ عَلَيْكُمْ نِعْمَتِي وَرَضِيتُ لَكُمُ ٱلْإِسْلَٰمَ دِينًا

...Today I have perfected your religion for you,
completed My favour to you, and have chosen Islam
for you as your religion... (al-Qur'an 5:3)

15

قَالَ رَسُولُ اللّهِ صَلَّى اللّهُ عَلَيْهِ وَسَلَّمَ: إِنَّ الدِّينَ يُسْرٌ وَلَنْ يُشَادَّ الدِّينَ أَحَدٌ إِلاَّ غَلَبَــهُ فَسَــدِّدُوا،

وَقَارِبُوا، وَأَبْشِرُوا، وَاسْتَعِينُوا بِالْغَدْوَةِ وَالرَّوْحَةِ وَشَيْءٍ مِنَ الدُّلْجَةِ. (البخاري)

THE PROPHET ﷺ said: 'The religion (of Islam) is easy. No one ever made it difficult without it becoming too much for him. So avoid extremes and strike a balance, do the best you can (in carrying out your religious observances) and be cheerful; and seek Allah's help (through prayer) in the morning and evening, and part of the night'. (*Bukhari*)

16

قَالَ رَسُولُ اللّهِ صَلَّى اللّهُ عَلَيْهِ وَسَلَّمَ: بُنِيَ الإِسْلَامُ عَلَى خَمْسٍ، شَهَادَةُ أَنْ لاَ إِلَهَ إِلاَّ اللّهُ، وَأَنَّ

مُحَمَّدًا رَسُولُ اللّهِ، وَإِقَامِ الصَّلاَةِ، وَإِيتَاءِ الزَّكَاةِ، وَالْحَجِّ، وَصَوْمِ رَمَضَانَ. (البخاري ومسلم)

THE PROPHET ﷺ said: 'Islam is built on five pillars:

* Bearing witness that there is no god but Allah (the One God), and that Muhammad is His Messenger.
* Establishing regular prayer.
* Paying the poor-due (zakat).
* Making pilgrimage (Hajj) to the House (of Allah in Makkah), and
* Fasting in (the month of) Ramadan'. (*Bukhari, Muslim*)

3

What is Faith?

إِنَّمَا ٱلْمُؤْمِنُونَ ٱلَّذِينَ إِذَا ذُكِرَ ٱللَّهُ وَجِلَتْ قُلُوبُهُمْ وَإِذَا تُلِيَتْ عَلَيْهِمْ
ءَايَٰتُهُۥ زَادَتْهُمْ إِيمَٰنًا وَعَلَىٰ رَبِّهِمْ يَتَوَكَّلُونَ ﴿٢﴾

The believers are those whose hearts tremble (with awe)
when Allah is mentioned; whose faith increases when His revelations are
recited to them, and who put their trust in their Lord. (al-Qur'an 8:2)

17

قَالَ رَسُولُ اللَّهِ صَلَّى اللَّهُ عَلَيْهِ وَسَلَّمَ: ..الإِيمَانُ أَنْ تُؤْمِنَ بِاللَّهِ، وَمَلاَئِكَتِهِ، وَكُتُبِهِ، وَرُسُلِهِ، وَالْيَوْمِ الآخِرِ، وَتُؤْمِنَ بِالْقَدَرِ خَيْرِهِ وَشَرِّهِ... والإِحْسَانُ أَنْ تَعْبُدَ اللَّهَ كَأَنَّكَ تَرَاهُ، فَإِنْ لَمْ تَكُنْ تَرَاهُ فَإِنَّهُ يَرَاكَ. (مسلم)

THE PROPHET ﷺ said: 'Faith is to believe in Allah, His angels, His Holy Books, His Messengers, the Day of Judgement, and to believe in Divine Destiny – the good and the bad... The highest degree of goodness is to worship Allah as though you see Him, and if you do not see Him, know that He sees you'. (*Muslim*)

18

عَنْ أَبِي أُمَامَةَ رَضِيَ اللَّهُ عَنْهُ أَنَّ رَجُلاً سَأَلَ رَسُولَ اللَّهِ صَلَّى اللَّهِ عَلَيْهِ وَسَلَّمَ مَا الإِيمَانُ؟ قَالَ: إِذَا سَرَّتْكَ حَسَنَتُكَ وَسَاءَتْكَ سَيِّئَتُكَ، فَأَنْتَ مُؤْمِنٌ. قَالَ يَا رَسُولَ اللَّهِ: فَمَا الإِثْمُ؟ قَالَ: إِذَا حَاكَ فِي نَفْسِكَ شَيْءٌ فَدَعْهُ. (أحمد)

ABU UMAMAH ﷺ related: 'A man once asked Allah's Messenger ﷺ, 'What is faith?' He replied: 'When your good deeds make you happy and your bad deeds make you sad, then you have faith.' Then the man asked him, 'What is sin?' The Prophet ﷺ replied: 'When anything troubles your conscience, stop doing it'. (*Ahmad*)

19

قَالَ رَسُولُ اللَّهِ صَلَّى اللَّهُ عَلَيْهِ وَسَلَّمَ: مَنْ رَأَى مِنْكُمْ مُنْكَرًا فَلْيُغَيِّرْهُ بِيَدِهِ، فَإِنْ لَمْ يَسْتَطِعْ فَبِلِسَانِهِ، فَإِنْ لَمْ يَسْتَطِعْ فَبِقَلْبِهِ، وَذَلِكَ أَضْعَفُ الْإِيمَانِ. (مسلم)

THE PROPHET ﷺ said: 'If any of you sees something bad, he should try to change it with his hand; if he cannot do that, then he should change it with his tongue; if he cannot do that, then he should detest it in his heart; and that is the weakest degree of faith'. (*Muslim*)

20

قَالَ رَسُولُ اللَّهِ صَلَّى اللَّهُ عَلَيْهِ وَسَلَّمَ: ثَلَاثٌ مَنْ كُنَّ فِيهِ وَجَدَ حَلَاوَةَ الْإِيمَان، أَنْ يَكُونَ اللَّهُ وَرَسُولُهُ أَحَبَّ إِلَيْهِ مِمَّا سِوَاهُمَا، وَأَنْ يُحِبَّ الْمَرْءَ لَا يُحِبُّهُ إِلاَّ لِلَّهِ، وَأَنْ يَكْرَهَ أَنْ يَعُودَ فِي الْكُفْرِ كَمَا يَكْرَهُ أَنْ يُقْذَفَ فِي النَّارِ. (البخاري ومسلم)

THE PROPHET ﷺ said: 'Whoever has three qualities will taste the sweetness of faith: To love Allah and His Messenger more than anything else; to love someone for Allah's sake alone, and to hate to return to unbelief just as much as one would hate to be thrown into a fire'. (*Bukhari, Muslim*)

The Qur'an

نَزَّلَ عَلَيْكَ ٱلْكِتَـٰبَ بِٱلْحَقِّ مُصَدِّقًا لِّمَا بَيْنَ يَدَيْهِ وَأَنزَلَ ٱلتَّوْرَىٰةَ وَٱلْإِنجِيلَ

مِن قَبْلُ هُدًى لِّلنَّاسِ وَأَنزَلَ ٱلْفُرْقَانَ ۗ ﴿٣﴾

He has revealed the Qur'an to you (step by step, O Muhammad) with truth,
confirming what was revealed before it, just as He revealed the Torah and
the Gospel before (this) as guidance for humanity… (al-Qur'an 3:3)

21

سَأَلَ الْحَارِثُ بْنُ هِشَامٍ رَضِيَ اللَّهُ عَنْهُ رَسُولَ اللَّهِ صَلَّى اللَّهُ عَلَيْهِ وَسَلَّمَ فَقَالَ: يَا رَسُولَ اللَّهِ كَيْفَ يَأْتِيكَ الْوَحْيُ؟ فَقَالَ رَسُولُ اللَّهِ صَلَّى اللَّهُ عَلَيْهِ وَسَلَّمَ: أَحْيَانًا يَأْتِينِي مِثْلَ صَلْصَلَةِ الْجَرَسِ، وَهُوَ أَشَدُّهُ عَلَيَّ فَيُفْصِمُ عَنِّي وَقَدْ وَعَيْتُ عَنْهُ مَا قَالَ، وَأَحْيَانًا يَتَمَثَّلُ لِيَ الْمَلَكُ رَجُلًا فَيُكَلِّمُنِي فَأَعِي مَا يَقُولُ. قَالَتْ عَائِشَةُ رَضِيَ اللَّهُ عَنْهَا: وَلَقَدْ رَأَيْتُهُ يَنْزِلُ عَلَيْهِ الْوَحْيُ فِي الْيَوْمِ الشَّدِيدِ الْبَرْدِ، فَيُفْصِمُ عَنْهُ وَإِنَّ جَبِينَهُ لَيَتَفَصَّدُ عَرَقًا. (البخاري)

AL-HARITH ibn Hisham ؓ asked the Prophet ﷺ: 'Messenger of Allah, how does revelation come to you?' The Prophet ﷺ replied, 'Sometimes it comes like the ringing of a bell. That is the hardest on me. Once that state passes I understand what was revealed. And at other times the Angel (Gabriel) comes in the form of a man and talks to me, and I understand what he says'. ʿA'ishah ؓ added: 'Truly, I saw the Prophet ﷺ after having received revelation on a very cold day and the sweat was dropping from his forehead'. (*Bukhari*)

22

قَالَ رَسُولُ اللَّهِ صَلَّى اللَّهُ عَلَيْهِ وَسَلَّمَ: إِنَّ أَفْضَلَكُمْ مَنْ تَعَلَّمَ الْقُرْآنَ وَعَلَّمَهُ. (البخاري)

THE PROPHET ﷺ said: 'The best of you are those who learn the Qur'an and teach it'. (*Bukhari*)

23

قَالَ رَسُولُ اللَّهِ صَلَّى اللَّهُ عَلَيْهِ وَسَلَّمَ: إِنَّ الَّذِي لَيْسَ فِي جَوْفِهِ شَيْءٌ مِنْ الْقُرْآنِ كَالْبَيْتِ الْخَرِبِ. (الترمذي)

THE PROPHET ﷺ said: 'A person who has not learned any of the Qur'an is like a house in ruins'. (*Tirmidhi*)

24

قَالَ رَسُولُ اللَّهِ صَلَّى اللَّهُ عَلَيْهِ وَسَلَّمَ: اقْرَءُوا الْقُرْآنَ فَإِنَّهُ يَأْتِي يَوْمَ الْقِيَامَةِ شَفِيعًا لِأَصْحَابِهِ. (مسلم)

THE PROPHET ﷺ said: 'Keep reading the Qur'an, for on the Day of Judgement it will come to intercede for those who read it regularly'. (*Muslim*)

25

قَالَ رَسُولُ اللَّهِ صَلَّى اللَّهُ عَلَيْهِ وَسَلَّمَ: يُقَالَ لِصَاحِبِ الْقُرْآنِ اقْرَأْ وَارْتَقِ، وَرَتِّلْ كَمَا كُنْتَ تُرَتِّلُ فِي الدُّنْيَا، فَإِنَّ مَنْزِلَتَكَ عِنْدَ آخِرِ آيَةٍ تَقْرَأُ بِهَا. (أبو داود والترمذي)

THE PROPHET ﷺ said: 'Someone who is in the habit of reciting the Qur'an will be told (on the Day of Judgement), 'Keep on reciting, and rising higher (in Paradise)! Recite as beautifully as you used to during your lifetime, for your station will be where the last verse of your recitation ends'. (*Abu Dawud, Tirmidhi*)

26

قَالَ رَسُولُ اللَّهِ صَلَّى اللَّهُ عَلَيْهِ وَسَلَّمَ: مَثَلُ الَّذِي يَقْرَأُ الْقُرْآنَ كَالْأُتْرُجَّةِ طَعْمُهَا طَيِّبٌ وَرِيحُهَا طَيِّبٌ. (البخاري)

THE PROPHET ﷺ said: 'A person who recites the Qur'an (regularly) is like the utrujjah fruit whose taste is delicious and smell is fragrant'. (*Bukhari*)

27

قَالَ رَسُولُ اللَّهِ صَلَّى اللَّهُ عَلَيْهِ وَسَلَّمَ: حَسِّنُوا الْقُرْآنَ بِأَصْوَاتِكُمْ، فَإِنَّ الصَّوْتَ الْحَسَنَ يَزِيدُ الْقُرْآنَ حُسْنًا. (الدارمي)

THE PROPHET ﷺ said: 'Beautify the Qur'an with your voices, for a beautiful voice increases the beauty of the Qur'an'. (*Darimi*)

28

قَالَ رَسُولُ اللَّهِ صَلَّى اللَّهُ عَلَيْهِ وَسَلَّمَ: الَّذِي يَقْرَأُ الْقُرْآنَ وَهُوَ مَاهِرٌ بِهِ فَهُوَ مَعَ السَّفَرَةِ الْكِرَامِ الْبَرَرَةِ، وَالَّذِي يَقْرَؤُهُ وَهُوَ يَشْتَدُّ عَلَيْهِ فَلَهُ أَجْرَانِ. (أحمد والدارمي)

THE PROPHET ﷺ said: 'Whoever recites the Qur'an with skill will be in the company of the noble and righteous emissaries (of God on the Last Day); and whoever recites the Qur'an with difficulty, making great effort, will have a double reward'. (*Ahmad, Darimi*)

5

Daily Prayers (Salat)

وَأَقِمِ ٱلصَّلَوٰةَ إِنَّ ٱلصَّلَوٰةَ تَنْهَىٰ عَنِ ٱلْفَحْشَاءِ وَٱلْمُنكَرِ

And establish regular prayer. Truly, prayer is a shield from indecency and sin... (al-Qur'an 29:45)

إِنَّ ٱلصَّلَوٰةَ كَانَتْ عَلَى ٱلْمُؤْمِنِينَ كِتَابًا مَّوْقُوتًا ۝

...Prayer has been appointed for the believers at fixed times. (al-Qur'an 4:103)

✳
29

قَالَ رَسُولُ اللَّهِ صَلَّى اللَّهُ عَلَيْهِ وَسَلَّمَ: مِفْتَاحُ الْجَنَّةِ الصَّلَاةُ، وَمِفْتَاحُ الصَّلَاةِ الطُّهُورُ. (أحمد)

THE PROPHET ﷺ said: 'The key to Paradise is the prayer (salat), and the key to the prayer is ritual purity (tuhur)'. (*Ahmad*)

✳
30

قَالَ رَسُولُ اللَّهِ صَلَّى اللَّهُ عَلَيْهِ وَسَلَّمَ: بَيْنَ الرَّجُلِ وَبَيْنَ الشِّرْكِ وَالْكُفْرِ تَرْكُ الصَّلَاةِ. (مسلم)

THE PROPHET ﷺ said: 'The difference between a believer and an idol-worshipper is abandoning the prayer'. (*Muslim*)

✳
31

قَالَ رَسُولُ اللَّهِ صَلَّى اللَّهُ عَلَيْهِ وَسَلَّمَ: أَرَأَيْتُمْ لَوْ أَنَّ نَهَرًا بِبَابِ أَحَدِكُمْ يَغْتَسِلُ فِيهِ كُلَّ يَوْمٍ خَمْسًا، مَا تَقُولُ ذَلِكَ يُبْقِي مِنْ دَرَنِهِ؟ قَالُوا: لَا يُبْقِي مِنْ دَرَنِهِ شَيْئًا. قَالَ: فَذَلِكَ مِثْلُ الصَّلَوَاتِ الْخَمْسِ، يَمْحُو اللَّهُ بِهِ الْخَطَايَا. (البخاري)

THE PROPHET ﷺ said: 'If one of you had a stream running at his door and he bathed in it five times every day, do you think any dirt would be left on him?' His Companions answered, 'No dirt at all would be left on him!' He said, 'That is what the five (daily) prayers are like, with which Allah washes away your sins'. (*Bukhari*)

✳

32

عَنْ عَبْدِ اللَّهِ بْنِ مَسْعُودٍ قَالَ سَأَلْتُ رَسُولَ اللَّهِ صَلَّى اللَّهُ عَلَيْهِ وَسَلَّمَ: أَيُّ الْعَمَلِ أَفْضَلُ؟ قَالَ:
الصَّلَاةُ لِوَقْتِهَا. (البخاري ومسلم)

'ABDULLAH ibn Mas'ud ﷺ said: 'I once asked Allah's Messenger ﷺ
which is the best of deeds. He replied, prayer at its correct time'.
(*Bukhari, Muslim*)

✳

33

قَالَ رَسُولُ اللَّهِ صَلَّى اللَّهُ عَلَيْهِ وَسَلَّمَ: صَلَاةُ الْجَمَاعَةِ تَفْضُلُ صَلَاةَ الْفَذِّ بِسَبْعٍ وَعِشْرِينَ دَرَجَةً.
(البخاري ومسلم)

THE PROPHET ﷺ said: 'Prayer offered in a Jama'ah (*Congregation*)
is twenty-seven times better than prayer that is performed alone'.
(*Bukhari, Muslim*)

✳

34

قَالَ رَسُولُ اللَّهِ صَلَّى اللَّهُ عَلَيْهِ وَسَلَّمَ: إِنَّ أَوَّلَ مَا يُحَاسَبُ بِهِ الْعَبْدُ يَوْمَ الْقِيَامَةِ مِنْ عَمَلِهِ صَلَاتُهُ،
فَإِنْ صَلُحَتْ فَقَدْ أَفْلَحَ وَأَنْجَحَ، وَإِنْ فَسَدَتْ فَقَدْ خَابَ وَخَسِرَ. (الترمذي)

THE PROPHET ﷺ said: 'The first deed that a person will be called to
account for on the Day of Judgement will be his prayers. If they are in
order he will be successful and prosper, but if they are not he will be
ruined and lost'. (*Tirmidhi*)

❋

35

قَالَ رَسُولُ اللَّهِ صَلَّى اللَّهُ عَلَيْهِ وَسَلَّمَ: مُرُوا أَوْلادَكُمْ بِالصَّلَاةِ وَهُمْ أَبْنَاءُ سَبْعِ سِنِينَ،
وَاضْرِبُوهُمْ عَلَيْهَا وَهُمْ أَبْنَاءُ عَشْرٍ. (أبو داود)

THE PROPHET ﷺ said: 'Teach your children to pray when they are seven, and discipline them when they are ten (if they do not do it)'. (*Abu Dawud*)

6

Personal Prayer (Du'a')

وَقَالَ رَبُّكُمُ ٱدْعُونِىٓ أَسْتَجِبْ لَكُمْ

Your Lord has said, Call on Me and I will answer you... (al-Qur'an 40:60)

36

قَالَ رَسُولُ اللّٰهِ صَلَّى اللّٰهُ عَلَيْهِ وَسَلَّمَ: الدُّعَاءُ مُخُّ الْعِبَادَةِ. (الترمذي)

THE PROPHET ﷺ said: 'Du'a' is the essence of worship'. (*Tirmidhi*)

37

قَالَ رَسُولُ اللّٰهِ صَلَّى اللّٰهُ عَلَيْهِ وَسَلَّمَ: مَنْ لَمْ يَسْأَلِ اللّٰهَ يَغْضَبْ عَلَيْهِ. (الترمذي)

THE PROPHET ﷺ said: 'Allah is angry with the person who never asks Him for anything'. (*Tirmidhi*)

38

قَالَ رَسُولُ اللّٰهِ صَلَّى اللّٰهُ عَلَيْهِ وَسَلَّمَ: مَا مِنْ أَحَدٍ يَدْعُو بِدُعَاءٍ إِلَّا آتَاهُ اللّٰهُ مَا سَأَلَ، أَوْ كَفَّ عَنْهُ مِنَ السُّوءِ مِثْلَهُ، مَا لَمْ يَدْعُ بِإِثْمٍ أَوْ قَطِيعَةِ رَحِمٍ. (الترمذي)

THE PROPHET ﷺ said: 'Whenever a Muslim asks Allah for anything, Allah will either grant his prayer or protect him from some harm, as long as he does not pray for something sinful or for something that would cut off family ties'. (*Tirmidhi*)

39

قَالَ رَسُولُ اللّٰهِ صَلَّى اللّٰهُ عَلَيْهِ وَسَلَّمَ: لَا يَقُولَنَّ أَحَدُكُمْ: اللّٰهُمَّ اغْفِرْ لِي إِنْ شِئْتَ، اللّٰهُمَّ ارْحَمْنِي إِنْ شِئْتَ، لِيَعْزِمِ الْمَسْأَلَةَ فَإِنَّهُ لَا مُكْرِهَ لَهُ. (البخاري ومسلم)

THE PROPHET ﷺ said: 'No one should pray saying, 'O Allah, forgive me if You will, have mercy on me if You will,' but he should ask with full confidence, for (in any case) no one can force Him'. (*Bukhari, Muslim*)

40

قَالَ رَسُولُ اللّٰهِ صَلَّى اللّٰهُ عَلَيْهِ وَسَلَّمَ: إِنَّ اللّٰهَ يَقُولُ: أَنَا عِنْدَ ظَنِّ عَبْدِي بِي، وَأَنَا مَعَهُ إِذَا دَعَانِي. (البخاري ومسلم)

THE PROPHET ﷺ said: 'Allah says, 'I am as My servant considers Me to be, and I am with him when he prays to Me'. (*Bukhari, Muslim*)

41

عَنِ ابْنِ عَبَّاسٍ رَضِيَ الله عَنْهُمَا قَالَ: كُنْتُ خَلْفَ رَسُولِ اللَّهِ صَلَّى اللَّهُ عَلَيْهِ وَسَلَّمَ يَوْمًا فَقَالَ لِي:
يَا غُلَامُ إِنِّي أُعَلِّمُكَ كَلِمَاتٍ، احْفَظِ اللَّهَ يَحْفَظْكَ، احْفَظِ اللَّهَ تَجِدْهُ تُجَاهَكَ، إِذَا سَأَلْتَ فَاسْأَلِ
اللَّهَ، وَإِذَا اسْتَعَنْتَ فَاسْتَعِنْ بِاللَّهِ، وَاعْلَمْ أَنَّ الْأُمَّةَ لَوِ اجْتَمَعَتْ عَلَى أَنْ يَنْفَعُوكَ بِشَيْءٍ لَمْ يَنْفَعُوكَ إِلَّا
بِشَيْءٍ قَدْ كَتَبَهُ اللَّهُ لَكَ، وَلَوِ اجْتَمَعُوا عَلَى أَنْ يَضُرُّوكَ بِشَيْءٍ لَمْ يَضُرُّوكَ إِلَّا بِشَيْءٍ قَدْ كَتَبَهُ اللَّهُ
عَلَيْكَ، رُفِعَتِ الْأَقْلَامُ وَجَفَّتِ الصُّحُفُ. (الترمذي و أحمد)

IBN ʿABBAS ﷺ said: 'One day I was mounted behind the Messenger of
Allah ﷺ (i.e. on his camel) when he said, 'Young man, I would like
to teach you something: Be mindful of Allah, and He will protect you.
Be mindful of Allah, and you will find Him in front of you. When you
ask (for anything), ask only from Him, and when you seek help, seek
help from Him. Know that if the entire world were to get together to
help you, they would only benefit you with something that Allah had
already destined for you. And if they were to combine (their efforts)
to harm you with anything, they could only harm you with something
that Allah had already written against you. The pens (of destiny) have
been lifted and the pages are dry.' (*Tirmidhi, Ahmad*)

7

Remembering Allah (Dhikr)

يَٰٓأَيُّهَا ٱلَّذِينَ ءَامَنُوا۟ ٱذْكُرُوا۟ ٱللَّهَ ذِكْرًا كَثِيرًا ۝ وَسَبِّحُوهُ بُكْرَةً وَأَصِيلًا ۝

O believers, remember Allah often;
and glorify His praises morning and evening. (al-Qur'an 33:41-42)

ٱلَّذِينَ ءَامَنُوا۟ وَتَطْمَئِنُّ قُلُوبُهُم بِذِكْرِ ٱللَّهِ

Surely in the remembrance of Allah do hearts find rest. (al-Qur'an 13:28)

42

قَالَ رَسُولُ اللَّهِ صَلَّى اللَّهُ عَلَيْهِ وَسَلَّمَ: سَبَقَ الْمُفَرِّدُونَ، سَبَقَ الْمُفَرِّدُونَ، قَالُوا: يَا رَسُولَ الله مَا الْمُفَرِّدُونَ؟ قَالَ: الذَّاكِرُونَ الله كَثِيراً وَالذَّاكِرَاتِ. (مسلم)

THE PROPHET ﷺ said: 'The mufarridun will win the race. The mufarridun will win the race.' People asked, 'Who are the mufarridun, O Messenger of Allah?' he replied. 'The men and women who remember Allah abundantly'. (*Muslim*)

43

جَاءَ أَعْرَابِيٌّ إِلَى رَسُولِ الله صَلَّى الله عَلَيْهِ وَسَلَّمَ وَقَالَ: إِنَّ شَرَائِعَ الإِسْلَامِ قَدْ كَثُرَتْ عَلَيَّ، فَأَخْبِرْنِي مِنْهَا بِشَيْءٍ أَتَشَبَّثُ بِهِ، قَالَ: لَا يَزَالُ لِسَانُكَ رَطْباً مِنْ ذِكْرِ الله. (الترمذي)

A MAN came to the Prophet ﷺ and said: 'O Messenger of Allah, the laws of Islam seem to be a lot for me (to remember), so tell me something that I should stick to.' He said, 'Let your tongue never cease to be moist with the remembrance of Allah'. (*Tirmidhi*)

44

قَالَ رَسُولُ اللَّهِ صَلَّى اللَّهُ عَلَيْهِ وَسَلَّمَ: لَا تُكْثِرُوا الْكَلَامَ بِغَيْرِ ذِكْرِ اللَّهِ، فَإِنَّ كَثْرَةَ الْكَلَامِ بِغَيْرِ ذِكْرِ اللَّهِ قَسْوَةٌ لِلْقَلْبِ، وَإِنَّ أَبْعَدَ النَّاسِ مِنَ اللَّهِ الْقَلْبُ الْقَاسِي. (الترمذي)

THE PROPHET ﷺ said: 'Do not talk too much without remembering and mentioning Allah, for too much talk without mentioning Allah hardens the heart, and the person farthest from Allah is the one with a hard heart'. (*Tirmidhi*)

45

قَالَ رَسُولُ اللَّهِ صَلَّى اللَّهُ عَلَيْهِ وَسَلَّمَ: مَثَلُ الَّذِي يَذْكُرُ رَبَّهُ وَالَّذِي لاَ يَذْكُرُهُ كَمَثَلِ الْحَيِّ وَالْمَيِّتِ

(البخاري)

THE PROPHET ﷺ said: 'He who remembers his Lord and he who does not are like the living and the dead'. (*Bukhari*)

46

قَالَ رَسُولُ اللَّهِ صَلَّى اللَّهُ عَلَيْهِ وَسَلَّمَ: لَا يَقْعُدُ قَوْمٌ يَذْكُرُونَ اللَّهَ عَزَّ وَجَلَّ، إِلَّا حَفَّتْهُمُ الْمَلَائِكَةُ، وَغَشِيَتْهُمُ الرَّحْمَةُ، وَنَزَلَتْ عَلَيْهِمُ السَّكِينَةُ، وَذَكَرَهُمُ اللَّهُ فِيمَنْ عِنْدَهُ. (مسلم)

THE PROPHET ﷺ said: 'Whenever a group gathers for remembering Allah, Mighty and Majestic is He, angels surround them, (Divine) mercy covers them, tranquillity descends on them, and Allah mentions them to those (angels) in His presence'. (*Muslim*)

8

Charity (Zakat and Sadaqah)

خُذْ مِنْ أَمْوَالِهِمْ صَدَقَةً تُطَهِّرُهُمْ وَتُزَكِّيهِم بِهَا

Collect a portion of their wealth in charity,
so that you may purify and bless them by means of it...(al-Qur'an 9:103)

وَمَآ أَنفَقْتُم مِّن شَيْءٍ فَهُوَ يُخْلِفُهُ ۖ وَهُوَ خَيْرُ الرَّزِقِينَ ۩

...Whatever you spend (in Allah's cause), He will replace it.
He is the Best of Providers. (al-Qur'an 34:39)

47

قَالَ رَسُولُ اللَّهِ صَلَّى اللَّهُ عَلَيْهِ وَسَلَّمَ: كُلُّ سُلَامَى عَلَيْهِ صَدَقَةٌ كُلَّ يَوْمٍ، يُعِينُ الرَّجُلَ فِي دَابَّتِهِ، يُحَامِلُهُ عَلَيْهَا أَوْ يَرْفَعُ عَلَيْهَا مَتَاعَهُ صَدَقَةٌ، وَالْكَلِمَةُ الطَّيِّبَةُ صَدَقَةٌ، وَكُلُّ خَطْوَةٍ يَمْشِيهَا إِلَى الصَّلَاةِ صَدَقَةٌ، وَدَلُّ الطَّرِيقِ صَدَقَةٌ. (البخاري ومسلم)

THE PROPHET ﷺ said: 'An act of charity is due every day from every joint of the body (as a means of showing gratitude to Allah for one's body and good health): Helping a person to ride his animal (or vehicle) or load his baggage is charity, a good word is charity, every step taken towards (the mosque for) prayer is charity, and showing someone the way is charity'. (*Bukhari, Muslim*)

48

قَالَ رَسُولُ اللَّهِ صَلَّى اللَّهُ عَلَيْهِ وَسَلَّمَ: كُلُّ مَعْرُوفٍ صَدَقَةٌ (البخاري ومسلم)

THE PROPHET ﷺ said: 'Every act of goodness is charity'. (*Bukhari, Muslim*)

49

قَالَ رَسُولُ اللَّهِ صَلَّى اللَّهُ عَلَيْهِ وَسَلَّمَ: لاَ تُوكِى فَيُوكَى عَلَيْكَ. (البخاري ومسلم)

THE PROPHET ﷺ said: 'Do not hold back (from giving to people and helping them), or Allah will withhold (His mercy and blessings) from you'. (*Bukhari, Muslim*)

50

قَالَ رَسُولُ اللَّهِ صَلَّى اللَّهُ عَلَيْهِ وَسَلَّمَ: مَا نَقَصَ مَالُ عَبْدٍ مِنْ صَدَقَةٍ. (الترمذي)

THE PROPHET ﷺ said: 'A person's wealth will never decrease from giving in charity'. (*Tirmidhi*)

9

The Fast of Ramadan

يَـٰٓأَيُّهَا ٱلَّذِينَ ءَامَنُوا۟ كُتِبَ عَلَيْكُمُ ٱلصِّيَامُ كَمَا كُتِبَ
عَلَى ٱلَّذِينَ مِن قَبْلِكُمْ لَعَلَّكُمْ تَتَّقُونَ ﴿١٨٣﴾

O believers, fasting is decreed for you as it was decreed for those before you,
so that you may (learn to) restrain yourselves. (al-Qur'an 2:183)

51

قَالَ رَسُولُ اللَّهِ صَلَّى اللَّهُ عَلَيْهِ وَسَلَّمَ: قَالَ اللَّهُ تَعَالَى: كُلُّ عَمَلِ ابْنِ آدَمَ لَهُ إِلَّا الصِّيَامَ فَإِنَّهُ لِي وَأَنَا أَجْزِي بِهِ... لِلصَّائِمِ فَرْحَتَانِ يَفْرَحُهُمَا، إِذَا أَفْطَرَ فَرِحَ، وَإِذَا لَقِيَ رَبَّهُ فَرِحَ بِصَوْمِهِ (البخاري ومسلم)

THE PROPHET ﷺ said: 'Allah has said: 'Every action of the son of Adam is for him except fasting, for that is solely for Me, and I shall reward it (in a special way)... A person who fasts experiences two joys, he is joyful when he breaks his fast, and he is joyful when he meets his Lord'. (*Bukhari, Muslim*)

52

قَالَ رَسُولُ اللَّهِ صَلَّى اللَّهُ عَلَيْهِ وَسَلَّمَ: مَنْ صَامَ رَمَضَانَ إِيمَانًا وَاحْتِسَابًا غُفِرَ لَهُ مَا تَقَدَّمَ مِنْ ذَنْبِهِ، وَمَنْ قَامَ لَيْلَةَ الْقَدْرِ إِيمَانًا وَاحْتِسَابًا غُفِرَ لَهُ مَا تَقَدَّمَ مِنْ ذَنْبِهِ. (البخاري ومسلم)

THE PROPHET ﷺ said: 'Whoever fasts during Ramadan with faith, seeking his reward from Allah, will have his past sins forgiven. And whoever spends the Night of Power[I] in prayer with faith, seeking his reward from Allah, will have his past sins forgiven'. (*Bukhari, Muslim*)

---

1. Laylat al-Qadr: the night of power when the Qur'an was first revealed. It falls on one of the last ten odd nights of Ramadan.

53

قَالَ رَسُولُ اللَّهِ صَلَّى اللَّهُ عَلَيْهِ وَسَلَّمَ: مَنْ قَامَ رَمَضَانَ إِيمَانًا وَاحْتِسَابًا غُفِرَ لَهُ مَا تَقَدَّمَ مِنْ ذَنْبِهِ. (البخاري ومسلم)

THE PROPHET ﷺ said: 'Whoever prays during the nights of Ramadan with faith, seeking his reward from Allah, will have his past sins forgiven'. (*Bukhari, Muslim*)

54

قَالَ رَسُولُ اللَّهِ صَلَّى اللَّهُ عَلَيْهِ وَسَلَّمَ: مَنْ لَمْ يَدَعْ قَوْلَ الزُّورِ وَالْعَمَلَ بِهِ، فَلَيْسَ لِلَّهِ حَاجَةٌ فِي أَنْ يَدَعَ طَعَامَهُ وَشَرَابَهُ. (البخاري ومسلم)

THE PROPHET ﷺ said: 'If a person does not give up accusations and bad behaviour while fasting, Allah has no need of his giving up food or drink'. (*Bukhari, Muslim*)

55

قَالَ رَسُولُ اللَّهِ صَلَّى اللَّهُ عَلَيْهِ وَسَلَّمَ: رُبَّ صَائِمٍ حَظُّهُ مِنْ صِيَامِهِ الْجُوعُ وَالْعَطَشُ، وَرُبَّ قَائِمٍ حَظُّهُ مِنْ قِيَامِهِ السَّهَرُ. (أحمد)

THE PROPHET ﷺ said: 'There are those who get nothing from their fast but hunger and thirst, and there are those who pray at night and get nothing from it but loss of sleep'. (*Ahmad*)

10

Pilgrimage to Makkah

وَلِلَّهِ عَلَى ٱلنَّاسِ حِجُّ ٱلْبَيْتِ مَنِ ٱسْتَطَاعَ إِلَيْهِ سَبِيلًا

…Pilgrimage to the House (at Makkah) is a duty that all people owe to Allah, if they are able to make the journey… (al-Qur'an 3:97)

ٱلْحَجُّ أَشْهُرٌ مَّعْلُومَٰتٌ فَمَن فَرَضَ فِيهِنَّ ٱلْحَجَّ فَلَا رَفَثَ
وَلَا فُسُوقَ وَلَا جِدَالَ فِى ٱلْحَجِّ

The pilgrimage is to be held in the well-known months.
Whoever intends to perform it at that time (should remember that) there
must not be any sexual contact or improper behaviour, nor abuse,
nor angry conversation while on the pilgrimage. (al-Qur'an 2:197)

56

سُئِلَ النَّبِيُّ صَلَّى اللَّهُ عَلَيْهِ وَسَلَّمَ أَيُّ الْأَعْمَالِ أَفْضَلُ؟ قَالَ: إِيمَانٌ بِاللَّهِ وَرَسُولِهِ، قِيلَ ثُمَّ مَاذَا؟ قَالَ جِهَادٌ فِي سَبِيلِ اللَّهِ، قِيلَ ثُمَّ مَاذَا؟ قَالَ حَجٌّ مَبْرُورٌ. (البخاري ومسلم)

THE PROPHET ﷺ was asked: 'What is the best deed'? He answered: 'Faith in Allah and His Messenger'. 'And after that'? he was asked. The Prophet ﷺ replied: 'To participate in jihad (striving with one's life and property in a just cause) for Allah's sake', 'And after that'? he was asked. He replied: 'To perform a pure Hajj (a Pilgrimage that is free from mistakes or sins)' (*Bukhari, Muslim*)

57

قَالَ رَسُولُ اللَّهِ صَلَّى اللَّهُ عَلَيْهِ وَسَلَّمَ: مَنْ حَجَّ هَذَا الْبَيْتَ فَلَمْ يَرْفُثْ وَلَمْ يَفْسُقْ، رَجَعَ كَيَوْمِ وَلَدَتْهُ أُمُّهُ. (البخاري ومسلم)

THE PROPHET ﷺ said: 'Whoever performs Hajj to this House (the Kaʿbah) without any obscenity or sin, returns as pure as (he was) on the day his mother gave birth to him'. (*Bukhari, Muslim*)

58

رَفَعَتِ امْرَأَةٌ صَبِيًّا لَهَا فَقَالَتْ يَا رَسُولَ اللَّهِ أَلِهَذَا حَجٌّ؟ قَالَ: نَعَمْ وَلَكِ أَجْرٌ. (مسلم)

A WOMAN once lifted a boy up to the Prophet ﷺ and asked: 'Can this (little) one perform Hajj'? 'Yes', he replied: 'and you will be rewarded for it'.[2] (*Muslim*)

---

2.   Someone who has made the pilgrimage as a child must repeat it as an adult, if he or she can afford to do so.

11

Good and Bad Deeds

وَلَا تَسْتَوِى ٱلْحَسَنَةُ وَلَا ٱلسَّيِّئَةُ ٱدْفَعْ بِٱلَّتِى هِىَ أَحْسَنُ فَإِذَا ٱلَّذِى
بَيْنَكَ وَبَيْنَهُۥ عَدَٰوَةٌ كَأَنَّهُۥ وَلِىٌّ حَمِيمٌ ﴿٣٤﴾
وَمَا يُلَقَّىٰهَآ إِلَّا ٱلَّذِينَ صَبَرُوا۟ وَمَا يُلَقَّىٰهَآ إِلَّا ذُو حَظٍّ عَظِيمٍ ﴿٣٥﴾

The good deed and the bad deed are not alike.
Repel the evil deed with one that is better, and then the one who was at
enmity with you (will become) a good friend.
But no one will attain this except those who patiently endure; and no one
will attain this except one who is truly fortunate. (al-Qur'an 41:34-35)

✳
59

قَالَ رَسُولُ اللَّهِ صَلَّى اللَّهُ عَلَيْهِ وَسَلَّمَ: الْبِرُّ حُسْنُ الْخُلُقِ، وَالْإِثْمُ مَا حَاكَ فِي صَدْرِكَ وَكَرِهْتَ أَنْ
يَطَّلِعَ عَلَيْهِ النَّاسُ (مسلم)

THE PROPHET ﷺ said: 'Righteousness is good character, and sin is what makes you uncomfortable inside, and you would not like other people to find out about'. (*Muslim*)

✳
60

قَالَ رَسُولُ اللَّهِ صَلَّى اللَّهُ عَلَيْهِ وَسَلَّمَ: دَعْ مَا يَرِيبُكَ إِلَى مَا لَا يَرِيبُكَ، فَإِنَّ الصِّدْقَ طُمَأْنِينَةٌ،
وَإِنَّ الْكَذِبَ رِيبَةٌ. (الترمذي والنسائي)

THE PROPHET ﷺ said: 'Leave whatever makes you doubt for what does not make you doubt; for it is truth that brings peace of mind, and falsehood that brings doubt'. (*Tirmidhi, Nasa'i*)

✳
61

قَالَ رَسُولُ اللَّهِ صَلَّى اللَّهُ عَلَيْهِ وَسَلَّمَ: اتَّقِ اللَّهَ حَيْثُمَا كُنْتَ، وَأَتْبِعِ السَّيِّئَةَ الْحَسَنَةَ تَمْحُهَا،
وَخَالِقِ النَّاسَ بِخُلُقٍ حَسَنٍ. (أحمد والترمذي)

THE PROPHET ﷺ said: 'Fear Allah wherever you are, follow up a bad deed with a good one and it will erase it, and behave well towards people'. (*Ahmad, Tirmidhi*)

✳
62

قَالَ رَسُولُ اللّٰهِ صَلَّى اللّٰهُ عَلَيْهِ وَسَلَّمَ: أَحَبُّ الْأَعْمَالِ إِلَى اللّٰهِ تَعَالَى أَدْوَمُهَا وَإِنْ قَلَّ.

(البخاري ومسلم)

THE PROPHET ﷺ said: 'The (good) deeds most loved by Allah are those that are done regularly, even if they are small'. (*Bukhari, Muslim*)

12

Reward and Punishment

مَنْ عَمِلَ سَيِّئَةً فَلَا يُجْزَىٰ إِلَّا مِثْلَهَا وَمَنْ عَمِلَ صَـٰلِحًا
مِّن ذَكَرٍ أَوْ أُنثَىٰ وَهُوَ مُؤْمِنٌ فَأُوْلَـٰٓئِكَ
يَدْخُلُونَ الْجَنَّةَ يُرْزَقُونَ فِيهَا بِغَيْرِ حِسَابٍ ﴿٤٠﴾

Whoever does an evil deed will only be repaid with one like it,
whereas whoever does a righteous deed, whether male or female,
and is a true believer, will enter Paradise. And they will be provided
for there abundantly, without measure. (al-Qur'an 40:40)

63

قَالَ رَسُولُ اللَّهِ صَلَّى اللَّهُ عَلَيْهِ وَسَلَّمَ: إِنَّمَا الْأَعْمَالُ بِالنِّيَّاتِ، وَإِنَّمَا لِكُلِّ امْرِئٍ مَا نَوَى.

(البخاري ومسلم)

THE PROPHET ﷺ said: 'Actions will be judged according to the intentions (behind them), and everyone will be repaid according to what he intended'. (*Bukhari, Muslim*)

64

قَالَ رَسُولُ اللَّهِ صَلَّى اللَّهُ عَلَيْهِ وَسَلَّمَ: إِنَّ اللَّهَ كَتَبَ الْحَسَنَاتِ وَالسَّيِّئَاتِ ثُمَّ بَيَّنَ ذَلِكَ، فَمَنْ هَمَّ بِحَسَنَةٍ فَلَمْ يَعْمَلْهَا كَتَبَهَا اللَّهُ لَهُ عِنْدَهُ حَسَنَةً كَامِلَةً، فَإِنْ هُوَ هَمَّ بِهَا فَعَمِلَهَا كَتَبَهَا اللَّهُ لَهُ عِنْدَهُ عَشْرَ حَسَنَاتٍ إِلَى سَبْعِ مِائَةِ ضِعْفٍ إِلَى أَضْعَافٍ كَثِيرَةٍ، وَمَنْ هَمَّ بِسَيِّئَةٍ فَلَمْ يَعْمَلْهَا كَتَبَهَا اللَّهُ لَهُ عِنْدَهُ حَسَنَةً كَامِلَةً، فَإِنْ هُوَ هَمَّ بِهَا فَعَمِلَهَا كَتَبَهَا اللَّهُ لَهُ سَيِّئَةً وَاحِدَةً. (البخاري ومسلم)

THE PROPHET ﷺ said: 'Allah records good and bad deeds (in this way): If anyone intends to do a good deed, but does not do it, Allah still records it with Him as one full good deed. If he intends a good deed and then carries it out, Allah records it with Him as ten to seven hundred times in reward or even increases it many times over. If anyone intends to do a bad deed but does not actually do it, Allah records it with Him as one full good deed. If he intends to do a bad deed and does it, Allah records it against him as (only) one bad deed'. (*Bukhari, Muslim*)

13

The Day of Judgement

اللَّهُ لَا إِلَٰهَ إِلَّا هُوَ لَيَجْمَعَنَّكُمْ إِلَىٰ يَوْمِ ٱلْقِيَٰمَةِ
لَا رَيْبَ فِيهِ ۗ وَمَنْ أَصْدَقُ مِنَ ٱللَّهِ حَدِيثًا ﴿٨٧﴾

Allah! There is no god but Him (the One God). He will gather you all
together (before Him) on the Day of Judgement; there is no doubt about it.
And whose word can be truer than Allah's? (al-Qur'an 4:87)

65

قَالَ رَسُولُ اللَّهِ صَلَّى اللَّهُ عَلَيْهِ وَسَلَّمَ: لَا تَزُولُ قَدَمَا عَبْدٍ يَوْمَ الْقِيَامَةِ حَتَّى يُسْأَلَ عَنْ عُمْرِه فِيمَا أَفْنَاهُ، وَعَنْ عِلْمِهِ مَا فَعَلَ بِهِ، وَعَنْ مَالِهِ مِنْ أَيْنَ اكْتَسَبَهُ وَفِيمَا أَنْفَقَهُ، وَعَنْ جِسْمِهِ فِيمَا أَبْلَاهُ.

(الترمذي والدارمي)

THE PROPHET ﷺ said: 'On the Day of Resurrection, every servant of Allah will remain standing (before Him) until he is questioned about his life, how he spent it; his knowledge, what he did with it; his money, how he earned it and spent it, and his body, how he used it'.
(*Tirmidhi and Darimi*)

۶۶

قَالَ رَسُولُ اللَّهِ صَلَّى اللَّهُ عَلَيْهِ وَسَلَّمَ: إِنَّ اللَّهَ عَزَّ وَجَلَّ يَقُولُ يَوْمَ الْقِيَامَةِ: يَا ابْنَ آدَمَ مَرِضْتُ
فَلَمْ تَعُدْنِي، قَالَ يَا رَبِّ كَيْفَ أَعُودُكَ وَأَنْتَ رَبُّ الْعَالَمِينَ، قَالَ أَمَا عَلِمْتَ أَنَّ عَبْدِي فُلَانًا
مَرِضَ فَلَمْ تَعُدْهُ، أَمَا عَلِمْتَ أَنَّكَ لَوْ عُدْتَهُ لَوَجَدْتَنِي عِنْدَهُ، يَا ابْنَ آدَمَ اسْتَطْعَمْتُكَ فَلَمْ تُطْعِمْنِي،
قَالَ يَا رَبِّ وَكَيْفَ أُطْعِمُكَ وَأَنْتَ رَبُّ الْعَالَمِينَ، قَالَ أَمَا عَلِمْتَ أَنَّهُ اسْتَطْعَمَكَ عَبْدِي فُلَانٌ فَلَمْ
تُطْعِمْهُ، أَمَا عَلِمْتَ أَنَّكَ لَوْ أَطْعَمْتَهُ لَوَجَدْتَ ذَلِكَ عِنْدِي، يَا ابْنَ آدَمَ اسْتَسْقَيْتُكَ فَلَمْ تَسْقِنِي،
قَالَ يَا رَبِّ كَيْفَ أَسْقِيكَ وَأَنْتَ رَبُّ الْعَالَمِينَ، قَالَ اسْتَسْقَاكَ عَبْدِي فُلَانٌ فَلَمْ تَسْقِهِ، أَمَا إِنَّكَ
لَوْ سَقَيْتَهُ لَوَجَدْتَ ذَلِكَ عِنْدِي. (مسلم)

THE PROPHET ﷺ said: 'On the Day of Judgement, Allah will say, 'O son of Adam, I was ill, and you did not visit Me.' The man will say, 'O my Lord, how could I visit You, when You are the Lord of all the Worlds?' Allah will say, 'Did you not know that My servant so-and-so was ill, and you did not visit him? 'Did you not know that if you had visited him you would have found Me with him'?

'O son of Adam, I asked you for food, and you did not feed Me.' The man will say, 'O my Lord, how could I feed You, when You are the Lord of all the Worlds?' Allah will say, 'Did you not know that My servant so-and-so asked you for food, and you did not feed him? Did you not know that if you had fed him you would have found (the reward for doing so) with Me'?

'O son of Adam, I asked you for a drink, and you did not give Me anything to drink.' The man will say, 'O my Lord, how could I give You something to drink, when You are the Lord of all the Worlds?' Allah will say, 'My servant so-and-so asked you for something to drink, and you did not give it to him. If you had given him something to drink you would have found (the reward for doing so) with Me'. (*Muslim*)

قَالَ رَسُولُ اللهِ صَلَّى اللَّهُ عَلَيْهِ وَسَلَّمَ: إِذَا اتُّخِذَ الْفَيْءُ دُوَلًا، وَالْأَمَانَةُ مَغْنَمًا، وَالزَّكَاةُ مَغْرَمًا، وَتُعُلِّمَ لِغَيْرِ الدِّينِ، وَأَطَاعَ الرَّجُلُ امْرَأَتَهُ وَعَقَّ أُمَّهُ، وَأَدْنَى صَدِيقَهُ وَأَقْصَى أَبَاهُ، وَظَهَرَتِ الْأَصْوَاتُ فِي الْمَسَاجِدِ، وَسَادَ الْقَبِيلَةَ فَاسِقُهُمْ، وَكَانَ زَعِيمُ الْقَوْمِ أَرْذَلَهُمْ، وَأُكْرِمَ الرَّجُلُ مَخَافَةَ شَرِّهِ، وَظَهَرَتِ الْقَيْنَاتُ وَالْمَعَازِفُ، وَشُرِبَتِ الْخُمُورُ، وَلَعَنَ آخِرُ هَذِهِ الْأُمَّةِ أَوَّلَهَا، فَلْيَرْتَقِبُوا عِنْدَ ذَلِكَ رِيحًا حَمْرَاءَ، وَزَلْزَلَةً وَخَسْفًا وَمَسْخًا وَقَذْفًا، وَآيَاتٍ تَتَابَعُ كَنِظَامٍ بَالٍ قُطِعَ سِلْكُهُ فَتَتَابَعَ. (الترمذي)

THE PROPHET ﷺ said: 'When booty is taken out of turn,
and the property given in trust is treated as spoils,
and the poor-due is regarded as a fine,
and knowledge is sought for non-religious reasons,
when a man obeys his wife but is undutiful towards his mother,
when he is close to his friend but distant from his father,
when voices are raised in the mosques,
when a corrupt member of a tribe becomes its chief,
and the most worthless member of a people becomes its leader,
when a man is shown honour out of fear of the evil that he may do,
when singing-girls and stringed instruments become popular,
and alcohol is drunk,
and when the last of this community (the Muslims)
curse the first of them –
Then let them look out for a red wind, earthquakes,
the earth splitting open;
changes in Allah's creation, pelting rain,
and signs following one another like pieces of a necklace falling one
after the other when its string is cut'. (*Tirmidhi*)

14

Paradise and Hell

فَأَمَّا مَن ثَقُلَتْ مَوَٰزِينُهُۥ ۝ فَهُوَ فِى عِيشَةٍ رَّاضِيَةٍ ۝
وَأَمَّا مَنْ خَفَّتْ مَوَٰزِينُهُۥ ۝ فَأُمُّهُۥ هَاوِيَةٌ ۝

As for the one whose balance (of good deeds) is heavy (on the scale),
he will live a pleasant life (in Paradise). But as for the one whose balance
(of good deeds) is light – he will have his home in Hell. (al-Qur'an 101:6-9)

68

قَالَ رَسُولُ اللَّهِ صَلَّى اللَّهُ عَلَيْهِ وَسَلَّمَ: تَحَاجَّتِ الْجَنَّةُ وَالنَّارُ، فَقَالَتِ النَّارُ أُوثِرْتُ بِالْمُتَكَبِّرِينَ وَالْمُتَجَبِّرِينَ، وَقَالَتِ الْجَنَّةُ مَا لِي لَا يَدْخُلُنِي إِلَّا ضُعَفَاءُ النَّاسِ وَسَقَطُهُمْ، قَالَ اللَّهُ تَبَارَكَ وَتَعَالَى لِلْجَنَّةِ أَنْتِ رَحْمَتِي أَرْحَمُ بِكِ مَنْ أَشَاءُ مِنْ عِبَادِي، وَقَالَ لِلنَّارِ إِنَّمَا أَنْتِ عَذَابِي أُعَذِّبُ بِكِ مَنْ أَشَاءُ مِنْ عِبَادِي، وَلِكُلٍّ وَاحِدَةٍ مِنْكُمَا مِلْؤُهَا. (البخاري ومسلم)

THE PROPHET ﷺ said: 'Paradise and Hellfire argued with one another. Hellfire said: 'In me are the proud and the tyrants.' Paradise replied, 'How is it that none enter me but the weak and lowly of mankind?' Allah, Blessed and Exalted is He, said to Paradise: 'You are My mercy, and through you I show mercy to whoever I will of My servants. And He said to Hellfire, 'You are My punishment. Through you I punish whoever I will of My servants; and it is for Me to see that each shall have its fill'. (*Bukhari, Muslim*)

69

قَالَ رَسُولُ اللَّهِ صَلَّى اللَّهُ عَلَيْهِ وَسَلَّمَ: لَوْ يَعْلَمُ الْمُؤْمِنُ مَا عِنْدَ اللَّهِ مِنَ الْعُقُوبَةِ مَا طَمِعَ بِجَنَّتِهِ أَحَدٌ، وَلَوْ يَعْلَمُ الْكَافِرُ مَا عِنْدَ اللَّهِ مِنَ الرَّحْمَةِ مَا قَنَطَ مِنْ جَنَّتِهِ أَحَدٌ. (مسلم)

THE PROPHET ﷺ said: 'If a believer realized how severe Allah's punishment will be, no one would dare hope for Paradise; and if an unbeliever realized how great Allah's mercy is, no one would lose hope of Paradise'. (*Muslim*)

70

قَالَ رَسُولُ اللَّهِ صَلَّى اللَّهُ عَلَيْهِ وَسَلَّمَ: الْجَنَّةُ أَقْرَبُ إِلَى أَحَدِكُمْ مِنْ شِرَاكِ نَعْلِهِ، وَالنَّارُ مِثْلُ ذَلِكَ. (البخاري)

THE PROPHET ﷺ said: 'Paradise is nearer to you than the tip of your sandals, and so is Hellfire'. (*Bukhari*)

71

قَالَ رَسُولُ اللَّهِ صَلَّى اللَّهُ عَلَيْهِ وَسَلَّمَ: مَنْ مَاتَ يُشْرِكُ بِاللَّهِ شَيْئًا دَخَلَ النَّارَ، وَمَنْ مَاتَ لَا يُشْرِكُ بِاللَّهِ شَيْئًا دَخَلَ الْجَنَّةَ. (مسلم)

THE PROPHET ﷺ said: 'Whoever dies worshipping other than Allah (the One God) will enter Hellfire and whoever dies not worshipping anything besides Allah will enter Paradise'. (*Muslim*)

72

قَالَ رَسُولُ اللَّهِ صَلَّى اللَّهُ عَلَيْهِ وَسَلَّمَ: مَفَاتِيحُ الْجَنَّةِ شَهَادَةُ أَنْ لَاإِلَهَ إِلاَّ الله (أحمد)

THE PROPHET ﷺ said: 'The keys to Paradise are to testify that there is no god but Allah (the One God)'. (*Ahmad*)

73

قَالَ رَسُولُ اللَّهِ صَلَّى اللَّهُ عَلَيْهِ وَسَلَّمَ: قَالَ اللَّهُ تَعَالَى أَعْدَدْتُ لِعِبَادِي الصَّالِحِينَ مَا لَا عَيْنٌ رَأَتْ،
وَلَا أُذُنٌ سَمِعَتْ، وَلَا خَطَرَ عَلَى قَلْبِ بَشَرٍ. (البخاري ومسلم)

THE PROPHET ﷺ said: 'Allah says: "I have prepared for My righteous servants (in Paradise such rewards) that no eye has ever seen and no ear has ever heard, and what has never occurred to the heart (or mind) of any human-being"'. (*Bukhari, Muslim*)

74

قَالَ رَسُولُ اللَّهِ صَلَّى اللَّهُ عَلَيْهِ وَسَلَّمَ: إِنَّ لِلَّهِ مِائَةَ رَحْمَةٍ أَنْزَلَ مِنْهَا رَحْمَةً وَاحِدَةً بَيْنَ الْجِنِّ وَالْإِنْسِ
وَالْبَهَائِمِ وَالْهَوَامِّ، فَبِهَا يَتَعَاطَفُونَ وَبِهَا يَتَرَاحَمُونَ، وَبِهَا تَعْطِفُ الْوَحْشُ عَلَى وَلَدِهَا، وَأَخَّرَ اللَّهُ تِسْعًا
وَتِسْعِينَ رَحْمَةً يَرْحَمُ بِهَا عِبَادَهُ يَوْمَ الْقِيَامَةِ. (البخاري ومسلم)

THE PROPHET ﷺ said: 'Allah has one hundred mercies. He has sent down one mercy for jinn and people and animals and insects, and with this they are kind to one another and feel empathy for one another, and wild animals care for their young. Allah has kept back (the remaining) ninety-nine mercies for the Day of Resurrection, and with them He will show mercy to His servants (by granting them Paradise)'. (*Bukhari, Muslim*)

15

Repentance

وَٱسْتَغْفِرُوا۟ رَبَّكُمْ ثُمَّ تُوبُوٓا۟ إِلَيْهِ إِنَّ رَبِّى رَحِيمٌ وَدُودٌ ۝

Seek your Lord's forgiveness and turn to Him in repentance,
for my Lord is indeed Most Merciful and Loving. (al-Qur'an 11:90)

75

قَالَ رَسُولُ اللَّهِ صَلَّى اللَّهُ عَلَيْهِ وَسَلَّمَ: قَالَ اللَّهُ تَبَارَكَ وَتَعَالَى: يَا ابْنَ آدَمَ إِنَّكَ مَا دَعَوْتَنِي وَرَجَوْتَنِي غَفَرْتُ لَكَ عَلَى مَا كَانَ فِيكَ وَلَا أُبَالِي، يَا ابْنَ آدَمَ لَوْ بَلَغَتْ ذُنُوبُكَ عَنَانَ السَّمَاءِ ثُمَّ اسْتَغْفَرْتَنِي غَفَرْتُ لَكَ وَلَا أُبَالِي، يَا ابْنَ آدَمَ إِنَّكَ لَوْ أَتَيْتَنِي بِقُرَابِ الْأَرْضِ خَطَايَا ثُمَّ لَقِيتَنِي لَا تُشْرِكُ بِي شَيْئًا لَأَتَيْتُكَ بِقُرَابِهَا مَغْفِرَةً. (الترمذي)

THE PROPHET ﷺ said: 'Allah, Blessed and Exalted is He, says, 'O son of Adam, as long as you call on Me and ask from Me, I shall forgive you for what you have done, and think nothing of it.

O son of Adam, even if your sins were to reach up to the clouds in the sky, and then you were to ask for My forgiveness, I would forgive you and think nothing of it.

O son of Adam, even if you were to come to Me with sins nearly as great as the earth, and then you were to meet Me (i.e. after death), not worshipping anything besides Me, I would bring you forgiveness nearly as great as the earth'. (*Tirmidhi*)

76

قَالَ رَسُولُ اللَّهِ صَلَّى اللَّهُ عَلَيْهِ وَسَلَّمَ: يَا أَيُّهَا النَّاسُ تُوبُوا إِلَى اللَّهِ فَإِنِّي أَتُوبُ فِي الْيَوْمِ إِلَيْهِ مِائَةَ مَرَّةٍ. (مسلم)

THE PROPHET ﷺ said: 'Turn to Allah (in repentance), O people, and ask for forgiveness (for your sins); for truly, I myself turn to Him in repentance one hundred times a day'. (*Muslim*)

77

قَالَ رَسُولُ اللَّهِ صَلَّى اللَّهُ عَلَيْهِ وَسَلَّمَ: كُلُّ بَنِي آدَمَ خَطَّاءٌ، وَخَيْرُ الْخَطَّائِينَ التَّوَّابُونَ.
(الترمذي وابن ماجه)

THE PROPHET said: 'All Children of Adam are prone to make mistakes, but the best of those who do wrong are those who constantly repent'.[3] (*Ibn Majah, Tirmidhi*)

THE PROPHET GAVE US MANY EXAMPLES OF HOW TO PRAY FOR FORGIVENESS.
HERE ARE TWO SIMPLE PRAYERS:

78

قَالَ رَسُولُ اللَّهِ صَلَّى اللَّهُ عَلَيْهِ وَسَلَّمَ: اللَّهُمَّ اغْفِرْ لِي ذَنْبِي كُلَّهُ، دِقَّهُ وَجِلَّهُ، وَأَوَّلَهُ وَآخِرَهُ،
وَعَلَانِيَتَهُ وَسِرَّهُ. (مسلم)

THE PROPHET said: 'O Allah, forgive all my sins – great and small, first and last, open and secret'. (*Muslim*)

79

عَنِ ابْنِ عُمَرَ رَضِيَ اللَّهُ عَنْهُ قَالَ إِنَّا كُنَّا لَنَعُدُّ لِرَسُولِ اللَّهِ صَلَّى اللَّهُ عَلَيْهِ وَسَلَّمَ فِي الْمَجْلِسِ
الْوَاحِدِ مِائَةَ مَرَّةٍ رَبِّ اغْفِرْ لِي وَتُبْ عَلَيَّ إِنَّكَ أَنْتَ التَّوَّابُ الرَّحِيمُ. (أبو داود)

IBN UMAR relates: 'We used to witness the Messenger of Allah, repeating one hundred times in one session: 'O Lord, forgive me and grant me repentance, for You are the Most Forgiving, the Most Merciful. (*Abu Dawud*)

---

3.   By making an intention not to repeat their sin, and seeking His forgiveness.

16

Kindness and Respect to Parents

وَقَضَىٰ رَبُّكَ أَلَّا تَعۡبُدُوٓاْ إِلَّآ إِيَّاهُ وَبِٱلۡوَٰلِدَيۡنِ إِحۡسَٰنًاۚ إِمَّا يَبۡلُغَنَّ عِندَكَ
ٱلۡكِبَرَ أَحَدُهُمَآ أَوۡ كِلَاهُمَا فَلَا تَقُل لَّهُمَآ أُفٍّ وَلَا تَنۡهَرۡهُمَا
وَقُل لَّهُمَا قَوۡلًا كَرِيمًا ٢٣ وَٱخۡفِضۡ لَهُمَا جَنَاحَ
ٱلذُّلِّ مِنَ ٱلرَّحۡمَةِ وَقُل رَّبِّ ٱرۡحَمۡهُمَا كَمَا رَبَّيَانِي صَغِيرًا ٢٤

Your Lord has decreed that you should worship none but Him,
and be good to your parents. If one or both of them reach old age during
your lifetime, do not say (as much as) 'Ugh!' to them, or scold them,
but speak to them with kindness and respect. And lower the wing of
humility to them, out of tenderness, and say, 'O Lord, have mercy on them,
even as they raised and cared for me when I was little.' (al-Qur'an 17:23-24)

80

جَاءَ رَجُلٌ إِلَى رَسُولِ اللَّهِ صَلَّى اللَّهُ عَلَيْهِ وَسَلَّمَ فَقَالَ: يَا رَسُولَ اللَّهِ مَنْ أَحَقُّ النَّاسِ بِحُسْنِ

صَحَابَتِي؟ قَالَ: أُمُّكَ قَالَ: ثُمَّ مَنْ؟ قَالَ: ثُمَّ أُمُّكَ؟ قَالَ: ثُمَّ مَنْ؟ قَالَ: ثُمَّ أُمُّكَ قَالَ: ثُمَّ مَنْ؟

قَالَ: ثُمَّ أَبُوكَ. وفي رواية أخرى ثُمَّ أَدْنَاكَ أَدْنَاكَ (البخاري ومسلم)

A MAN once came to the Prophet ﷺ and asked: 'O Messenger of Allah, who of all people most deserves good company from me? 'Your mother,' he replied. 'Then who?' the man asked. 'Your mother,' the Prophet replied. 'Then who?' the man asked a third time. 'Your mother,' the Prophet replied once again. 'Then who?' the man persisted. 'Your father.' Another version adds: 'And then your close relatives'. (*Bukhari, Muslim*)

81

قَالَ رَسُولُ اللَّهِ صَلَّى اللَّهُ عَلَيْهِ وَسَلَّمَ: رِضَى الرَّبِّ فِي رِضَى الْوَالِدِ، وَسَخَطُ الرَّبِّ فِي سَخَطِ

الْوَالِدِ. (الترمذي)

THE PROPHET ﷺ said: 'The Lord (Allah) is pleased when the parent is pleased, and He is displeased when the parent is displeased'. (*Tirmidhi*)

قَالَ رَسُولُ اللَّهِ صَلَّى اللَّهُ عَلَيْهِ وَسَلَّمَ: لَاطَاعَةَ لِمَخْلُوقٍ فِي مَعْصِيَةِ الْخَالِقِ (البغوي)

THE PROPHET ﷺ said: 'No creature should be obeyed if it involves disobeying the Creator'. (*Baghawi*)

قَالَ رَسُولُ اللَّهِ صَلَّى اللَّهُ عَلَيْهِ وَسَلَّمَ: إِنَّ مِنْ أَكْبَرِ الْكَبَائِرِ أَنْ يَلْعَنَ الرَّجُلُ وَالِدَيْهِ، قِيلَ يَا رَسُولَ اللَّهِ وَكَيْفَ يَلْعَنُ الرَّجُلُ وَالِدَيْهِ؟ قَالَ يَسُبُّ الرَّجُلُ أَبَا الرَّجُلِ فَيَسُبُّ أَبَاهُ وَيَسُبُّ أُمَّهُ. (البخاري)

THE PROPHET ﷺ said: 'One of the greatest sins is for a man to curse his parents. (His Companions were shocked at this.) They asked, 'Who would curse his (own) parents?' The Prophet ﷺ answered, 'Yes, when a man insults the father of another man, and he in turn insults his father and mother'. (*Bukhari*)

🞧 84

أَتَى رَجُلٌ النَّبِيَّ صَلَّى اللّٰهُ عَلَيْهِ وَسَلَّمَ فَقَالَ: إِنِّي جِئْتُ أُبَايِعُكَ عَلَى الْهِجْرَةِ وَلَقَدْ تَرَكْتُ أَبَوَيَّ

يَبْكِيَانِ قَالَ: ارْجِعْ إِلَيْهِمَا فَأَضْحِكْهُمَا كَمَا أَبْكَيْتَهُمَا. (النسائي وأحمد)

A MAN came to the Prophet ﷺ and said: 'I have come to join in the hijrah (to Madinah) but I have left my parents weeping.' The Prophet ﷺ said: 'Go back to them and make them laugh as you have made them weep'. (*Nasa'i and Ahmad*)

🞧 85

قَالَ رَسُولَ اللّٰهِ صَلَّى اللّٰهُ عَلَيْهِ وَسَلَّمَ: رَغِمَ أَنْفُ، ثُمَّ رَغِمَ أَنْفُ، ثُمَّ رَغِمَ أَنْفُ، قِيلَ مَنْ يَا رَسُولَ

اللّٰهِ؟ قَالَ: مَنْ أَدْرَكَ أَبَوَيْهِ عِنْدَ الْكِبَرِ أَحَدَهُمَا أَوْ كِلَيْهِمَا فَلَمْ يَدْخُلِ الْجَنَّةَ. (مسلم)

THE PROPHET ﷺ once exclaimed, 'May his nose be rubbed in dust! May his nose be rubbed in dust! May his nose by rubbed in dust! He was asked, 'Who, O Messenger of Allah?' He replied, 'Anyone who is still alive when one or both of his parents reach old age yet he does not enter Paradise (as a result of caring for and serving them)'! (*Muslim*)

17

Kindness to Relatives

وَٱعْبُدُوا۟ ٱللَّهَ وَلَا تُشْرِكُوا۟ بِهِۦ شَيْـًٔا ۖ وَبِٱلْوَٰلِدَيْنِ إِحْسَٰنًا وَبِذِى ٱلْقُرْبَىٰ

Serve Allah and do not worship anything besides Him, and show
kindness to your parents and near relatives... (al-Qur'an 4:36)

86

قَالَ رَسُولُ الله صَلَّى اللهُ عَلَيْهِ وَسَلَّمَ: خَيْرُكُمْ خَيْرُكُمْ لِأَهْلِهِ، وَأَنَا خَيْرُكُمْ لِأَهْلِي.

(الترمذي، وابن ماجه)

THE PROPHET ﷺ said: 'The best of you is the one who is best to his own family, and I am the best of you towards my family'.
(*Tirmidhi, Ibn Majah*)

87

قَالَ رَسُولُ اللَّهِ صَلَّى اللهُ عَلَيْهِ وَسَلَّمَ: مَنْ كَانَ يُؤْمِنُ بِالله وَالْيَوْمِ الآخِرِ فَلْيَصِلْ رَحِمَهُ. (مسلم)

THE PROPHET ﷺ said: 'Whoever believes in Allah and the Last Day should maintain close ties with his relatives'. (*Muslim*)

88

قَالَ رَسُولَ اللَّهِ صَلَّى اللهُ عَلَيْهِ وَسَلَّمَ: مَنْ أَحَبَّ أَنْ يُبْسَطَ لَهُ فِي رِزْقِهِ، وَيُنْسَأَ لَهُ فِي أَثَرِهِ، فَلْيَصِلْ رَحِمَهُ. (البخاري ومسلم)

THE PROPHET ﷺ said: 'Whoever would like to be given more provision (by Allah in this life) and would like to be remembered well by future generations should maintain strong family ties'. (*Bukhari, Muslim*)

❋

89

قَالَ رَسُولُ اللَّهِ صَلَّى اللَّهُ عَلَيْهِ وَسَلَّمَ: لَيْسَ مِنَّا مَنْ لَمْ يَرْحَمْ صَغِيرَنَا وَيُوَقِّرْ كَبِيرَنَا. (الترمذي)

THE PROPHET ﷺ said: 'He is not one of us who does not show mercy to our little ones and respect to our elders'. (*Tirmidhi*)

❋

90

سُئِلَتْ عَائِشَةُ رَضِيَ اللَّهُ عَنْهَا عَنْ مَا كَانَ النَّبِيُّ صَلَّى اللَّهُ عَلَيْهِ وَسَلَّمَ يَصْنَعُ فِي بَيْتِهِ فَقَالَتْ: كَانَ يَكُونُ فِي مِهْنَةِ أَهْلِهِ، تَعْنِي خِدْمَةَ أَهْلِهِ، فَإِذَا حَضَرَتْ الصَّلَاةُ خَرَجَ إِلَى الصَّلَاةِ. (البخاري)

ʿAʾISHAH ﷺ was asked: 'What did the Prophet ﷺ used to do at home?' She answered, 'He kept himself busy with helping the members of his household, and when the time for prayer came, he would go out for the prayer'. (*Bukhari*)

18

Treatment of Children

رَبَّنَا هَبْ لَنَا مِنْ أَزْوَاجِنَا وَذُرِّيَّـٰتِنَا قُرَّةَ أَعْيُنٍ
وَاجْعَلْنَا لِلْمُتَّقِينَ إِمَامًا ﴿٧٤﴾

...O Lord, grant us wives and children who will be the comfort of our eyes,
and make us good examples for the righteous... (al-Qur'an 25:74)

91

قَالَ رَسُولُ اللَّهِ صَلَّى اللَّهُ عَلَيْهِ وَسَلَّمَ: مَنْ وُلِدَ لَهُ وَلَدٌ فَلْيُحْسِنِ اسْمَهُ وَأَدَبَهُ. (البيهقي)

THE PROPHET ﷺ said: 'He who is blessed with a child should give him/her a good name and teach him/her good manners'. (*Bayhaqi*)

92

قَالَ رَسُولُ اللَّهِ صَلَّى اللَّهُ عَلَيْهِ وَسَلَّمَ: مَا نَحَلَ وَالِدٌ وَلَداً مِنْ نَحْلٍ أَفْضَلَ مِنْ أَدَبٍ حَسَنٍ. (الترمذي)

THE PROPHET ﷺ said: 'There is no better gift a parent can give his child than good manners'. (*Tirmidhi*)

93

قَالَ رَسُولُ اللَّهِ صَلَّى اللَّهُ عَلَيْهِ وَسَلَّمَ: مَنْ عَالَ ثَلَاثَ بَنَاتٍ فَأَدَّبَهُنَّ وَزَوَّجَهُنَّ وَأَحْسَنَ إِلَيْهِنَّ فَلَهُ الْجَنَّةُ. (أبو داود)

THE PROPHET ﷺ said: 'If anyone cares for three daughters, gives them a good upbringing, marries them (to good husbands) and treats them well, he will enter Paradise'. (*Abu Dawud*)

94

قَالَ رَسُولُ اللَّهِ صَلَّى اللَّهُ عَلَيْهِ وَسَلَّمَ: أَفْضَلُ دِينَارٍ يُنْفِقُهُ الرَّجُلُ، دِينَارٌ يُنْفِقُهُ عَلَى عِيَالِهِ. (مسلم)

THE PROPHET ﷺ said: 'The best money is that which a man spends on the members of his family'. (*Muslim*)

95

قَالَ رَسُولُ اللَّهِ صَلَّى اللَّهُ عَلَيْهِ وَسَلَّمَ: مَنْ فَرَّقَ بَيْنَ الْوَالِدَةِ وَوَلَدِهَا فَرَّقَ الله بَيْنَهُ وَبَيْنَ أَحِبَّتِهِ يَوْمَ الْقِيَامَةِ. (الترمذي والدارمي)

THE PROPHET ﷺ said: 'If anyone separates a mother from her child, Allah will separate him from those he loves on the Day of Resurrection'. (*Tirmidhi, Darimi*)

96

قَبَّلَ رَسُولُ اللَّهِ صَلَّى اللَّهُ عَلَيْهِ وَسَلَّمَ الْحَسَنَ بْنَ عَلِيٍّ وَعِنْدَهُ الْأَقْرَعُ بْنُ حَابِسٍ التَّمِيمِيُّ جَالِسًا فَقَالَ الْأَقْرَعُ: إِنَّ لِي عَشَرَةً مِنَ الْوَلَدِ مَا قَبَّلْتُ مِنْهُمْ أَحَدًا، فَنَظَرَ إِلَيْهِ رَسُولُ اللَّهِ صَلَّى اللَّهُ عَلَيْهِ وَسَلَّمَ ثُمَّ قَالَ: مَنْ لَا يَرْحَمْ لَا يُرْحَمْ. (البخاري)

ALLAH'S MESSENGER ﷺ once kissed his grandson Hasan while a man named al-Aqraʿ ibn Habis al-Tamimi was sitting beside him. The man said, 'I have ten children and I have never kissed any of them.' The Prophet ﷺ looked at him (sadly) and said, 'Whoever does not show mercy will not be shown mercy'. (*Bukhari*)

97

عَنِ النُّعْمَانِ بْنِ بَشِيرٍ رَضِيَ اللَّهُ عَنْهُ أَنَّ أَبَاهُ أَتَى بِهِ إِلَى رَسُولِ اللَّهِ صَلَّى اللَّهُ عَلَيْهِ وَسَلَّمَ فَقَالَ إِنِّي نَحَلْتُ ابْنِي هَذَا غُلَامًا، فَقَالَ: أَكُلَّ وَلَدِكَ نَحَلْتَ مِثْلَهُ، قَالَ: لَا، قَالَ: اتَّقُوا اللَّهَ وَاعْدِلُوا فِي أَوْلَادِكُمْ. (البخاري ومسلم)

NUʿMAN ibn Bashir ﷺ said that his father once brought him to the Messenger of Allah ﷺ and said, 'I have given a slave boy (as a gift) to this son of mine.' The Prophet ﷺ asked, 'Have you done the same for all of your children?' and he replied that he had not. The Prophet then said, 'Fear Allah, and be fair to all your children'. (*Bukhari, Muslim*)

98

عَنْ مُعَاذٍ رَضِيَ اللَّهُ عَنْهُ قَالَ أَوْصَانِي رَسُولُ اللَّهِ صَلَّى اللَّهُ عَلَيْهِ وَسَلَّمَ بِعَشْرِ كَلِمَاتٍ... وَأَنْفِقْ عَلَى عِيَالِكَ مِنْ طَوْلِكَ، وَلَا تَرْفَعْ عَنْهُمْ عَصَاكَ أَدَبًا، وَأَخِفْهُمْ فِي اللَّهِ. (أحمد)

MUʿADH ﷺ said: 'Allah's Messenger ﷺ instructed me to do ten things (three of which were); '... Spend on your children according to what you can afford. Do not hesitate to discipline them in the course of their upbringing, and instil in them the fear of Allah'. (*Ahmad*)

19

Respect for Elders and Teachers

فَسْـَٔلُوٓا۟ أَهْلَ ٱلذِّكْرِ إِن كُنتُمْ لَا تَعْلَمُونَ ۝

Ask the people of knowledge (who remember Allah much),
if you do not know. (al-Qur'an 21:7)

99

قَالَ رَسُولُ اللَّهِ صَلَّى اللَّهُ عَلَيْهِ وَسَلَّمَ: مَا أَكْرَمَ شَابٌّ شَيْخًا لِسِنِّهِ إِلَّا قَيَّضَ اللَّهُ لَهُ مَنْ يُكْرِمُهُ عِنْدَ سِنِّهِ. (الترمذي)

THE PROPHET ﷺ said: 'Whenever a young person honours an old man because of his age, Allah will give him someone to honour him when he is old'. (*Tirmidhi*)

100

قَالَ رَسُولُ اللَّهِ صَلَّى اللَّهُ عَلَيْهِ وَسَلَّمَ: كَانَ إِبْرَاهِيمُ صَلَّى اللَّهُ عَلَيْهِ وَسَلَّمَ أَوَّلَ النَّاسِ رَأَى الشَّيْبَ فَقَالَ: يَا رَبِّ مَا هَذَا؟ فَقَالَ اللَّهُ تَبَارَكَ وَتَعَالَى: وَقَارٌ يَا إِبْرَاهِيمُ فَقَالَ يَا رَبِّ زِدْنِي وَقَارًا. (مالك)

THE PROPHET Ibrahim ﷺ (Abraham) was the first person to see grey hair. He inquired, 'O Lord, what is this?' Allah, Blessed and Exalted is He, said, 'It is a sign of dignity, O Ibrahim.' 'O Lord, increase me in dignity,' he replied'. (*Malik*)

101

قَالَ رَسُولَ اللَّهِ صَلَّى اللَّهُ عَلَيْهِ وَسَلَّمَ: إِنَّمَا بُعِثْتُ مُعَلِّمًا. (الدارمي)

THE PROPHET ﷺ said: 'Truly, I have been sent as a teacher'. (*Darimi*)

102

عَنْ مُعَاوِيَةَ بْنِ الْحَكَمِ السُّلَمِيِّ قَالَ: بِأَبِي هُوَ وَأُمِّي مَا رَأَيْتُ مُعَلِّمًا قَبْلَهُ وَلَا بَعْدَهُ أَحْسَنَ تَعْلِيمًا مِنْهُ فَوَاللَّهِ مَا كَهَرَنِي وَلَا ضَرَبَنِي وَلَا شَتَمَنِي. (الدارمي)

MUʿAWIYAH ibn al-Hakam al-Sulami ﷺ said: 'By my father and mother, (I swear that) I never saw a teacher, before or after him, who was a better teacher than the Messenger of Allah ﷺ. By God, he never shouted at me, or punished me, or insulted me'. (*Darimi*)

20

Leadership and Authority

يَٰٓأَيُّهَا ٱلَّذِينَ ءَامَنُوٓاْ أَطِيعُواْ ٱللَّهَ وَأَطِيعُواْ ٱلرَّسُولَ وَأُوْلِي ٱلْأَمْرِ
مِنكُمْ فَإِن تَنَٰزَعْتُمْ فِى شَىْءٍ فَرُدُّوهُ إِلَى ٱللَّهِ وَٱلرَّسُولِ إِن كُنتُمْ
تُؤْمِنُونَ بِٱللَّهِ وَٱلْيَوْمِ ٱلْأَخِرِ ذَٰلِكَ خَيْرٌ وَأَحْسَنُ تَأْوِيلًا ﴿٥٩﴾

    O believers, obey Allah, and obey the Messenger and those who are in positions of authority among you. And if you disagree on some matter, refer it to Allah and His Messenger, if you believe in Allah and the Last Day. That is a better and more suitable way to reach a final decision. (al-Qur'an 4:59)

103

قَالَ رَسُولُ اللَّهِ صَلَّى اللَّهُ عَلَيْهِ وَسَلَّمَ: السَّمْعُ وَالطَّاعَةُ عَلَى الْمَرْءِ الْمُسْلِمِ فِيمَا أَحَبَّ وَكَرِهَ،
مَا لَمْ يُؤْمَرْ بِمَعْصِيَةٍ، فَإِذَا أُمِرَ بِمَعْصِيَةٍ فَلَا سَمْعَ وَلَا طَاعَةَ. (البخاري ومسلم)

THE PROPHET ﷺ said: 'A Muslim must hear and obey (those in authority), whether he likes the order or not – unless he is asked to do something sinful, in which case he need not hear or obey'. (*Bukhari, Muslim*)

104

قَالَ رَسُولُ اللَّهِ صَلَّى اللَّهُ عَلَيْهِ وَسَلَّمَ: إِذَا خَرَجَ ثَلَاثَةٌ فِي سَفَرٍ فَلْيُؤَمِّرُوا أَحَدَهُمْ. (أبو داود)

THE PROPHET ﷺ said: 'When three (or more) people set out on a journey they should choose one of them to be their leader'. (*Abu Dawud*)

105

قَالَ رَسُولُ اللَّهِ صَلَّى اللَّهُ عَلَيْهِ وَسَلَّمَ: لَا تَسْأَلِ الْإِمَارَةَ فَإِنَّكَ إِنْ أُوتِيتَهَا عَنْ مَسْأَلَةٍ وُكِّلْتَ إِلَيْهَا،
وَإِنْ أُوتِيتَهَا مِنْ غَيْرِ مَسْأَلَةٍ أُعِنْتَ عَلَيْهَا. (البخاري ومسلم)

THE PROPHET ﷺ said: 'Do not ask to be made a leader, for if the position is given to you after you have asked for it you will be left on your own to carry it out. However, if it is given to you without asking, you will be helped (by Allah) in carrying out its duties'. (*Bukhari, Muslim*)

21

Neighbours and Guests

وَٱعۡبُدُواْ ٱللَّهَ وَلَا تُشۡرِكُواْ بِهِۦ شَيۡـًٔا وَبِٱلۡوَٰلِدَيۡنِ إِحۡسَٰنًا وَبِذِى ٱلۡقُرۡبَىٰ

وَٱلۡيَتَٰمَىٰ وَٱلۡمَسَٰكِينِ وَٱلۡجَارِ ذِى ٱلۡقُرۡبَىٰ وَٱلۡجَارِ ٱلۡجُنُبِ

And worship Allah and do not join any partners with Him
and show kindness to your parents and near relatives, to the orphans
and those in need and to the neighbour who is of your own people
as well as the neighbour who is a stranger... (al-Qur'an 4:36)

106

قَالَ رَسُولُ اللَّهِ صَلَّى اللَّهُ عَلَيْهِ وَسَلَّمَ: وَاللَّهِ لَا يُؤْمِنُ، وَاللَّهِ لَا يُؤْمِنُ، وَاللَّهِ لَا يُؤْمِنُ (قَالَهَا ثَلَاثَ

مَرَّاتٍ) قَالُوا وَمَا ذَاكَ يَا رَسُولَ اللَّهِ؟ قَالَ: الْجَارُ لَا يَأْمَنُ الْجَارُ بَوَائِقَهُ، قَالُوا: وَمَا بَوَائِقُهُ؟

قَالَ: شَرُّهُ. (أحمد)

THE PROPHET ﷺ said: 'By Allah, he is not a believer! By Allah he is not a believer! By Allah he is not a believer!' He was asked, 'Who, O Messenger of Allah?' he replied, 'Anyone whose neighbour does not feel safe from his harm'. (*Ahmad*)

107

قَالَ رَسُولُ اللَّهِ صَلَّى اللَّهُ عَلَيْهِ وَسَلَّمَ: مَنْ كَانَ يُؤْمِنُ بِاللَّهِ وَالْيَوْمِ الْآخِرِ فَلَا يُؤْذِ جَارَهُ، وَمَنْ كَانَ

يُؤْمِنُ بِاللَّهِ وَالْيَوْمِ الْآخِرِ فَلْيُكْرِمْ ضَيْفَهُ، وَمَنْ كَانَ يُؤْمِنُ بِاللَّهِ وَالْيَوْمِ الْآخِرِ فَلْيَقُلْ خَيْرًا أَوْ لِيَصْمُتْ.

(البخاري ومسلم)

THE PROPHET ﷺ said: 'Whoever believes in Allah and the Last Day should not trouble his neighbour, and whoever believes in Allah and the Last Day should entertain his guest generously, and whoever believes in Allah and the Last Day should say what is good, or be silent'. (*Bukhari, Muslim*)

108

قَالَ رَسُولُ اللَّهِ صَلَّى اللَّهُ عَلَيْهِ وَسَلَّمَ: الِاسْتِئْذَانُ ثَلَاثٌ، فَإِنْ أُذِنَ لَكَ وَإِلَّا فَارْجِعْ. (الترمذي)

THE PROPHET ﷺ said: 'Ask permission to enter (someone's home) up to three times. If you are given permission (you may enter). Otherwise, you should leave'. (*Tirmidhi*)

109

عَنْ عَائِشَةَ رَضِيَ اللَّهُ عَنْهَا قَالَتْ: قُلْتُ يَا رَسُولَ اللَّهِ إِنَّ لِي جَارَيْنِ فَإِلَى أَيِّهِمَا أُهْدِي؟ قَالَ: إِلَى أَقْرَبِهِمَا مِنْكِ بَابًا. (البخاري)

'A'ISHAH ﷺ relates: 'I said: "O Messenger of Allah, I have two neighbours. Which of them should I give gifts to (first)"? He replied: 'To the one whose door is nearer to yours'. (*Bukhari*)

110

قَالَ رَسُولُ اللَّهِ صَلَّى اللَّهُ عَلَيْهِ وَسَلَّمَ: مَا زَالَ يُوصِينِي جِبْرِيلُ بِالْجَارِ حَتَّى ظَنَنْتُ أَنَّهُ سَيُوَرِّثُهُ. (البخاري)

THE PROPHET ﷺ said: '(The angel) Gabriel kept on advising me about the (importance of) being good to neighbours, until I thought he would order me to give them a share of my inheritance'. (*Bukhari*)

22

Friendship

إِنَّمَا وَلِيُّكُمُ ٱللَّهُ وَرَسُولُهُۥ وَٱلَّذِينَ ءَامَنُوا ٱلَّذِينَ يُقِيمُونَ
ٱلصَّلَوٰةَ وَيُؤْتُونَ ٱلزَّكَوٰةَ وَهُمْ رَٰكِعُونَ ۝

Your true friends and protectors are Allah and His Messenger,
and those who believe: (those) who establish regular prayer and pay the
poor-due, and bow down (humbly in prayer). (al-Qur'an 5:55)

111

قَالَ رَسُولُ اللّٰهِ صَلَّى اللّٰهُ عَلَيْهِ وَسَلَّمَ: الْمَرْءُ عَلَى دِينِ خَلِيلِهِ، فَلْيَنْظُرْ أَحَدُكُمْ مَنْ يُخَالِلْ. (أحمد)

THE PROPHET ﷺ said: 'A person tends to follow the faith (and lifestyle) of his friends, so be careful who you make friends with'. (*Ahmad*)

112

قَالَ رَسُولُ اللّٰهِ صَلَّى اللّٰهُ عَلَيْهِ وَسَلَّمَ مَثَلُ الْجَلِيسِ الصَّالِحِ وَالْجَلِيسِ السَّوْءِ كَحَامِلِ الْمِسْكِ وَنَافِخِ الْكِيرِ فَحَامِلُ الْمِسْكِ إِمَّا أَنْ يُحْذِيَكَ وَإِمَّا أَنْ تَبْتَاعَ مِنْهُ وَإِمَّا أَنْ تَجِدَ مِنْهُ رِيحًا طَيِّبَةً وَنَافِخُ الْكِيرِ إِمَّا أَنْ يُحْرِقَ ثِيَابَكَ وَإِمَّا أَنْ تَجِدَ رِيحًا خَبِيثَةً. (البخاري ومسلم)

THE PROPHET ﷺ said: 'A good friend and a bad friend are like a perfume-seller and a blacksmith: The perfume-seller might give you some perfume as a gift, or you might buy some from him, or at least you might smell its fragrance. As for the blacksmith, he might singe your clothes, and at the very least you will breathe in the fumes of the furnace'. (*Bukhari, Muslim*)

⚜ 113

قَالَ رَسُولُ اللَّهِ صَلَّى اللَّهُ عَلَيْهِ وَسَلَّمَ: إِنَّ أَحَدَكُمْ مِرْآةُ أَخِيهِ، فَإِنْ رَأَى بِهِ أَذًى فَلْيُمِطْهُ عَنْهُ. (الترمذي)

THE PROPHET ﷺ said: 'Each of you is the mirror of his brother, so if he sees any blemish in him, he should wipe it away from him'. (*Tirmidhi*)

⚜ 114

قَالَ رَسُولُ اللَّهِ صَلَّى اللَّهُ عَلَيْهِ وَسَلَّمَ: إِذَا أَحَبَّ أَحَدُكُمْ أَخَاهُ فَلْيُعْلِمْهُ إِيَّاهُ. (ابو داود والترمذي)

THE PROPHET ﷺ said: 'If a person loves his brother, he should tell him so'. (*Abu Dawud, Tirmidhi*)

23

Brotherhood

إِنَّمَا ٱلْمُؤْمِنُونَ إِخْوَةٌ فَأَصْلِحُوا بَيْنَ أَخَوَيْكُمْ وَٱتَّقُوا ٱللَّهَ لَعَلَّكُمْ تُرْحَمُونَ ﴿١٠﴾

The believers are nothing else than brothers (in faith).
So make peace between your brothers; and fear Allah,
in order that you may receive mercy. (al-Qur'an 49:10)

115

قَالَ رَسُولُ اللَّهِ صَلَّى اللَّهُ عَلَيْهِ وَسَلَّمَ: لَا يُؤْمِنُ أَحَدُكُمْ حَتَّى يُحِبَّ لِأَخِيهِ مَا يُحِبُّ لِنَفْسِهِ. (مسلم)

THE PROPHET ﷺ said: 'None of you is truly a believer until he wishes for his brother what he wishes for himself'. (*Muslim*)

116

قَالَ رَسُولُ اللَّهِ صَلَّى اللَّهُ عَلَيْهِ وَسَلَّمَ: يَا أَيُّهَا النَّاسُ، أَلَا إِنَّ رَبَّكُمْ وَاحِدٌ، وَإِنَّ أَبَاكُمْ وَاحِدٌ، أَلَا لَا فَضْلَ لِعَرَبِيٍّ عَلَى أَعْجَمِيٍّ، وَلَا لِعَجَمِيٍّ عَلَى عَرَبِيٍّ، وَلَا لِأَحْمَرَ عَلَى أَسْوَدَ، وَلَا أَسْوَدَ عَلَى أَحْمَرَ، إِلَّا بِالتَّقْوَى. (أحمد)

THE PROPHET ﷺ said: 'O people, your Lord is One and your ancestor (Adam) is one. There is no superiority for an Arab over a non-Arab, nor for a non-Arab over an Arab, nor for a fair-skinned person over a person with dark skin, nor for a dark-skinned person over a person with fair skin. Whoever is more pious and God-fearing is more deserving of honour'. (*Ahmad*)

117

قَالَ رَسُولُ اللَّهِ صَلَّى اللَّهُ عَلَيْهِ وَسَلَّمَ: مَنْ نَفَّسَ عَنْ مُؤْمِنٍ كُرْبَةً مِنْ كُرَبِ الدُّنْيَا نَفَّسَ اللَّهُ عَنْهُ كُرْبَةً مِنْ كُرَبِ يَوْمِ الْقِيَامَةِ، وَمَنْ يَسَّرَ عَلَى مُعْسِرٍ يَسَّرَ اللَّهُ عَلَيْهِ فِي الدُّنْيَا وَالْآخِرَةِ، وَمَنْ سَتَرَ مُسْلِمًا سَتَرَهُ اللَّهُ فِي الدُّنْيَا وَالْآخِرَةِ. (مسلم والترمذي)

THE PROPHET ﷺ said: 'Whoever fulfils the needs of his brother, Allah will fulfil his needs on the Day of Resurrection; whoever eases his brother's difficulty, Allah will ease his difficulty in this life and on the Day of Resurrection; and whoever covers up (the hidden faults of) a Muslim, Allah will cover his hidden faults (from the view of other people) in this life and the hereafter'. (*Muslim, Tirmidhi*)

118

قَالَ رَسُولُ اللَّهِ صَلَّى اللَّهُ عَلَيْهِ وَسَلَّمَ: لَا يَحِلُّ لِمُسْلِمٍ أَنْ يَهْجُرَ أَخَاهُ فَوْقَ ثَلَاثٍ، يَلْتَقِيَانِ فَيَصُدُّ هَذَا، وَيَصُدُّ هَذَا، وَخَيْرُهُمَا الَّذِي يَبْدَأُ بِالسَّلَامِ. (البخاري)

THE PROPHET ﷺ said: 'It is unlawful for a Muslim to avoid and refuse to speak to his fellow Muslim for more than three (days). (It is unlawful for them to behave in such a way) that when they meet, one of them turns his face away from the other, and the other turns his face from the first. The better of the two is the one who greets the other first with salam'. (*Bukhari*)

※
119

قَالَ رَسُولُ اللَّهِ صَلَّى اللَّهُ عَلَيْهِ وَسَلَّمَ: انْصُرْ أَخَاكَ ظَالِمًا أَوْ مَظْلُومًا، فَقَالَ رَجُلٌ: يَا رَسُولَ اللَّهِ
أَنْصُرُهُ إِذَا كَانَ مَظْلُومًا، أَفَرَأَيْتَ إِذَا كَانَ ظَالِمًا كَيْفَ أَنْصُرُهُ؟ قَالَ تَحْجُزُهُ أَوْ تَمْنَعُهُ مِنَ الظُّلْمِ
فَإِنَّ ذَلِكَ نَصْرُهُ. (البخاري)

THE PROPHET ﷺ said: 'Help your brother whether he does wrong, or is wronged. A man asked, 'O Messenger of Allah! I will help him if he is wronged, but how can I help him if he does something wrong?'
The Prophet ﷺ replied, 'By preventing him from his wrongdoing, for that is helping him'. (*Bukhari*)

※
120

قَالَ رَسُولُ اللَّهِ صَلَّى اللَّهُ عَلَيْهِ وَسَلَّمَ: الْمُسْلِمُ أَخُو الْمُسْلِمِ، لَا يَظْلِمُهُ وَلَا يَخْذُلُهُ وَلَا يَحْقِرُهُ،
التَّقْوَى هَاهُنَا –وَيُشِيرُ إِلَى صَدْرِهِ ثَلَاثَ مَرَّاتٍ– بِحَسْبِ امْرِئٍ مِنَ الشَّرِّ أَنْ يَحْقِرَ أَخَاهُ الْمُسْلِمَ،
كُلُّ الْمُسْلِمِ عَلَى الْمُسْلِمِ حَرَامٌ، دَمُهُ وَمَالُهُ وَعِرْضُهُ. (مسلم)

THE PROPHET ﷺ said: 'A Muslim is the brother of a Muslim. He does not oppress him, abandon him, or look down on him. Righteousness is here,' he said, and he pointed towards his chest three times. 'It is bad enough for a Muslim to look down on his fellow Muslim. A Muslim should consider that everything that belongs to his brother has a special, protected status: his blood, his wealth and his honour'. (*Muslim*)

24

Knowledge

قُلْ هَلْ يَسْتَوِى ٱلَّذِينَ يَعْلَمُونَ وَٱلَّذِينَ لَا يَعْلَمُونَ

Are those who know equal to those who do not? (al-Qur'an 39:9)

قُل رَّبِّ زِدْنِي عِلْمًا ۝

Say, 'O Lord, increase me in knowledge.' (al-Qur'an 20:114)

121

قَالَ رَسُولُ اللَّهِ صَلَّى اللَّهُ عَلَيْهِ وَسَلَّمَ: طَلَبُ الْعِلْمِ فَرِيضَةٌ عَلَى كُلِّ مُسْلِمٍ. (ابن ماجه والبيهقي)

THE PROPHET ﷺ said: 'Seeking knowledge is a religious obligation for every Muslim (male and female)'. (*Ibn Majah, Bayhaqi*)

122

قَالَ رَسُولُ اللَّهِ صَلَّى اللَّهُ عَلَيْهِ وَسَلَّمَ: تَعَلَّمُوا الْعِلْمَ وَعَلِّمُوهُ النَّاسَ، تَعَلَّمُوا الْفَرَائِضَ وَعَلِّمُوهَا النَّاسَ، تَعَلَّمُوا الْقُرْآنَ وَعَلِّمُوهُ النَّاسَ. (الدارمي)

THE PROPHET ﷺ said: 'Acquire knowledge, and teach it to people; learn your religious obligations and teach them to people; learn the Qur'an and teach it to people'. (*Darimi*)

123

قَالَ رَسُولُ اللَّهِ صَلَّى اللَّهُ عَلَيْهِ وَسَلَّمَ: فَضْلُ الْعَالِمِ عَلَى الْعَابِدِ كَفَضْلِي عَلَى أَدْنَاكُمْ، وَإِنَّ اللَّهَ وَمَلَائِكَتَهُ وَأَهْلَ السَّمَوَاتِ وَالْأَرَضِينَ، حَتَّى النَّمْلَةَ فِي جُحْرِهَا، وَحَتَّى الْحُوتُ لَيُصَلُّونَ عَلَى مُعَلِّمِ النَّاسِ الْخَيْرَ. (الترمذي)

THE PROPHET ﷺ said: 'A religious scholar is as far above an (ignorant) worshipper as I am above the rest of you. Truly, Allah, His angels and all those in the heavens and the earth – even the ants in their anthills and the fish – invoke blessings on those who instruct others in anything that is good'. (*Tirmidhi*)

124

قَالَ رَسُولُ اللَّهِ صَلَّى اللَّهُ عَلَيْهِ وَسَلَّمَ: إِنَّ اللَّهَ لَا يَقْبِضُ الْعِلْمَ انْتِزَاعًا يَنْتَزِعُهُ مِنَ الْعِبَادِ، وَلَكِنْ يَقْبِضُ الْعِلْمَ بِقَبْضِ الْعُلَمَاءِ، حَتَّى إِذَا لَمْ يُبْقِ عَالِمًا اتَّخَذَ النَّاسُ رُءُوسًا جُهَّالًا، فَسُئِلُوا فَأَفْتَوْا بِغَيْرِ عِلْمٍ، فَضَلُّوا وَأَضَلُّوا. (البخاري)

THE PROPHET ﷺ said: 'Allah will not take away (religious) knowledge by removing it from people's hearts, but He will take it away by the death of scholars, until, when no (true) scholars remain, people will take the ignorant (among them) as their leaders. When they are consulted, they will give their verdicts without knowledge. So they will go astray and will lead people astray'. (*Bukhari*)

25

Work

فَإِذَا قُضِيَتِ ٱلصَّلَوٰةُ فَٱنتَشِرُوا۟ فِى ٱلْأَرْضِ وَٱبْتَغُوا۟
مِن فَضْلِ ٱللَّهِ وَٱذْكُرُوا۟ ٱللَّهَ كَثِيرًا لَّعَلَّكُمْ تُفْلِحُونَ ﴿١٠﴾

Then when the prayer is finished, spread out through the land and seek
Allah's bounty (through work or trade), and remember Allah much so that
you may be successful. (al-Qur'an 62:10)

125

قِيلَ يَا رَسُولَ اللّٰهِ أَيُّ الْكَسْبِ أَطْيَبُ؟ قَالَ: عَمَلُ الرَّجُلِ بِيَدِهِ، وَكُلُّ بَيْعٍ مَبْرُورٍ. (أحمد)

ALLAH'S MESSENGER ﷺ was asked what type of earning was best.
He replied: 'A man's work with his hands, and any decent business'.
(*Ahmad*)

126

قَالَ رَسُولُ اللّٰهِ صَلَّى اللّٰهُ عَلَيْهِ وَسَلَّمَ: مَا أَكَلَ أَحَدٌ طَعَامًا قَطُّ خَيْرًا مِنْ أَنْ يَأْكُلَ مِنْ عَمَلِ يَدِهِ،
وَإِنَّ نَبِيَّ اللّٰهِ دَاوُدَ عَلَيْهِ السَّلَام كَانَ يَأْكُلُ مِنْ عَمَلِ يَدِهِ. (البخاري)

THE PROPHET ﷺ said: 'No one eats better food than what he earns
with his own hands. The Prophet Dawud ﷺ used to eat from what he
earned by the work of his hands'. (*Bukhari*)

127

قَالَ رَسُولُ اللّٰهِ صَلَّى اللّٰهُ عَلَيْهِ وَسَلَّمَ: نِعْمَ الْمَالُ الصَّالِحُ لِلْمَرْءِ الصَّالِحِ. (أحمد)

THE PROPHET ﷺ said: 'How good is the wealth it is that is earned
honourably by a righteous person'! (*Ahmad*)

128

قَالَ رَسُولُ اللهِ صَلَّى اللهُ عَلَيْهِ وَسَلَّمَ: وَلَا فَتَحَ عَبْدٌ بَابَ مَسْأَلَةٍ إِلَّا فَتَحَ اللهُ عَلَيْهِ بَابَ فَقْرٍ.
(الترمذي)

THE PROPHET ﷺ said: 'Whenever somebody opens for himself the door of begging, Allah opens for him the door of poverty'. (*Tirmidhi*)

129

أَتَتْ فَاطِمَةُ رَضِيَ اللهُ عَنْهَا النَّبِيَّ صَلَّى اللهُ عَلَيْهِ وَسَلَّمَ تَسْأَلُهُ خَادِمًا فَقَالَ: أَلَا أُخْبِرُكِ مَا هُوَ خَيْرٌ لَكِ مِنْهُ، تُسَبِّحِينَ اللهَ عِنْدَ مَنَامِكِ ثَلَاثًا وَثَلَاثِينَ، وَتَحْمَدِينَ اللهَ ثَلَاثًا وَثَلَاثِينَ، وَتُكَبِّرِينَ اللهَ أَرْبَعًا وَثَلَاثِينَ. (البخاري)

FATIMAH ﵂ (the Prophet's daughter) came to her father ﷺ (after she was married) and asked him for a servant (to help with her housework). The Prophet ﷺ said, 'Shall I not inform you of something that is better for you than a servant? Recite: 'Subhanallah (Glory be to Allah' thirty-three times, Al-hamdulillah (Praise be to Allah) thirty three times, and Allahu Akbar (Allah is Great) thirty-four times before you go to bed'. (*Bukhari*)

26

Treatment of Animals
and the Environment

وَمَا مِن دَآبَّةٍ فِى ٱلْأَرْضِ وَلَا طَٰٓئِرٍ يَطِيرُ بِجَنَاحَيْهِ إِلَّا أُمَمٌ أَمْثَالُكُم

There is not an animal (living) on the earth, nor a creature
that flies with two wings which does not belong to a community
like you (humans). (al-Qur'an 6:38)

130

قَالَ رَسُولَ اللَّهِ صَلَّى اللَّهُ عَلَيْهِ وَسَلَّمَ: إِنَّ الدُّنْيَا خَضِرَةٌ حُلْوَةٌ، وَإِنَّ اللَّهَ مُسْتَخْلِفُكُمْ فِيهَا، فَنَاظِرٌ

كَيْفَ تَعْمَلُونَ (مسلم)

THE PROPHET ﷺ said: 'The world is green and delightful, and Allah has put you in charge of it and is watching how you behave'. (*Muslim*)

131

عَنْ عَائِشَةَ رَضِيَ الله عَنْهَا قَالَتْ: كُنْتُ عَلَى بَعِيرٍ صَعْبٍ فَجَعَلْتُ أَضْرِبُهُ، فَقَالَ لِي رَسُولُ

الله صَلَّى الله عَلَيْهِ وَسَلَّمَ: عَلَيْكِ بِالرِّفْقِ، فَإِنَّ الرِّفْقَ لَا يَكُونُ فِي شَيْءٍ إِلَّا زَانَهُ وَلَا يُنْزَعُ مِنْ

شَيْءٍ إِلَّا شَانَهُ. (أحمد)

'A'ISHAH ﷺ said: 'I was once riding a difficult (slow moving) camel, so I kept hitting it. When the Prophet ﷺ saw me, he said: Be gentle, for gentleness adorns everything in which it is found, and its absence leaves everything tainted'. (*Ahmad*)

132

عَنْ عَبْدِ اللهِ بْنِ مَسْعُودٍ قَالَ: كُنَّا مَعَ رَسُولِ اللهِ صَلَّى اللهُ عَلَيْهِ وَسَلَّمَ فِي سَفَرٍ فَانْطَلَقَ لِحَاجَتِهِ،
فَرَأَيْنَا حُمَرَةً مَعَهَا فَرْخَانِ، فَأَخَذْنَا فَرْخَيْهَا فَجَاءَتِ الْحُمَرَةُ فَجَعَلَتْ تَفْرُشُ، فَجَاءَ النَّبِيُّ صَلَّى اللهُ
عَلَيْهِ وَسَلَّمَ فَقَالَ: مَنْ فَجَعَ هَذِهِ بِوَلَدِهَا؟، رُدُّوا وَلَدَهَا إِلَيْهَا، وَرَأَى قَرْيَةَ نَمْلٍ قَدْ حَرَّقْنَاهَا، فَقَالَ
مَنْ حَرَّقَ هَذِهِ؟ قُلْنَا: نَحْنُ، قَالَ: إِنَّهُ لَا يَنْبَغِي أَنْ يُعَذِّبَ بِالنَّارِ إِلَّا رَبُّ النَّارِ. (أبو داود)

ABDULLAH ibn Mas'ūd ﷺ reports: 'We were travelling with Allah's Messenger ﷺ (…when) we saw a humarah bird with her two chicks, and we captured her chicks. The mother bird came and began to flutter her wings. Then the Prophet ﷺ came and said, "Who has made this bird miserable by snatching her chicks? Return her chicks to her". He also saw an ant colony that we had burnt. He asked, "Who has burnt this?" "We did", we replied. He said, "It is not right for anyone but the Lord of fire to punish with fire"'. (*Abu Dawud*)

133

قَالَ رَسُولُ اللهِ صَلَّى اللهُ عَلَيْهِ وَسَلَّمَ: مَنْ قَتَلَ عُصْفُورًا عَبَثًا عَجَّ إِلَى اللهِ عَزَّ وَجَلَّ يَوْمَ الْقِيَامَةِ،
يَقُولُ يَا رَبِّ إِنَّ فُلَانًا قَتَلَنِي عَبَثًا وَلَمْ يَقْتُلْنِي لِمَنْفَعَةٍ. (النسائي)

THE PROPHET ﷺ said: 'Anyone who kills even a sparrow for no reason (should know that) it will cry aloud to Allah on the Day of Resurrection, saying, 'O my Lord! So-and-so killed me just for fun; he killed me for no good reason'! (*Nasa'i*)

134

قَالَ رَسُولَ اللَّهِ صَلَّى اللَّهُ عَلَيْهِ وَسَلَّمَ: لَا تَتَّخِذُوا شَيْئًا فِيهِ الرُّوحُ غَرَضًا. (مسلم)

THE PROPHET ﷺ said: 'Do not use any living thing as a target'. (*Muslim*)

135

قَالَ رَسُولَ اللَّهِ صَلَّى اللَّهُ عَلَيْهِ وَسَلَّمَ: إِنَّ اللَّهَ كَتَبَ الْإِحْسَانَ عَلَى كُلِّ شَيْءٍ.. إِذَا ذَبَحْتُمْ فَأَحْسِنُوا الذَّبْحَ، وَلْيُحِدَّ أَحَدُكُمْ شَفْرَتَهُ فَلْيُرِحْ ذَبِيحَتَهُ. (مسلم)

THE PROPHET ﷺ said: 'Allah has commanded excellence in all things…
If you slaughter, slaughter well. The one who slaughters should
sharpen his blade and spare suffering to the animal'. (*Muslim*)

136

قَالَ رَسُولُ اللَّهِ صَلَّى اللَّهُ عَلَيْهِ وَسَلَّمَ: مَا مِنْ مُسْلِمٍ يَغْرِسُ غَرْسًا، أَوْ يَزْرَعُ زَرْعًا، فَيَأْكُلُ مِنْهُ طَيْرٌ أَوْ إِنْسَانٌ أَوْ بَهِيمَةٌ، إِلَّا كَانَ لَهُ بِهِ صَدَقَةٌ. (مسلم)

THE PROPHET ﷺ said: 'If a Muslim plants a seedling or cultivates a
field, whenever a bird, a human or an animal eats of it, it will be
counted as charity for him'. (*Muslim*)

27

Good Manners and Character

إِنَّ ٱللَّهَ يَأْمُرُ بِٱلْعَدْلِ وَٱلْإِحْسَٰنِ وَإِيتَآئِ ذِى ٱلْقُرْبَىٰ وَيَنْهَىٰ عَنِ ٱلْفَحْشَآءِ وَٱلْمُنكَرِ وَٱلْبَغْىِ يَعِظُكُمْ لَعَلَّكُمْ تَذَكَّرُونَ ﴿٩٠﴾

Allah commands justice and goodness, and generosity to one's relatives,
and forbids any kind of indecency, wrongdoing or oppression.
He warns you so that you might take heed. (al-Qur'an 16:90)

137

قَالَ رَسُولُ اللّٰهِ صَلَّى اللّٰهُ عَلَيْهِ وَسَلَّمَ: إِنَّمَا بُعِثْتُ لِأُتَمِّمَ مَكَارِمَ الْأَخْلَاقِ. (أحمد ومالك)

THE PROPHET ﷺ said: 'Surely, I was sent to perfect the qualities of righteous character'. (*Ahmad, Malik*)

Consideration for Others

138

قَالَ رَسُولُ اللّٰهِ صَلَّى اللّٰهُ عَلَيْهِ وَسَلَّمَ: ارْحَمُوا مَنْ فِي الْأَرْضِ يَرْحَمْكُمْ مَنْ فِي السَّمَاءِ. (الترمذي)

THE PROPHET ﷺ said: Show mercy to people on earth so that He who is in heaven will have mercy on you'. (*Tirmidhi*)

139

قَالَ رَسُولُ اللّٰهِ صَلَّى اللّٰهُ عَلَيْهِ وَسَلَّمَ: مَنْ لَمْ يَشْكُرِ النَّاسَ لَمْ يَشْكُرِ اللّٰهَ عَزَّ وَجَلَّ. (أحمد والترمذي)

THE PROPHET ﷺ said: 'Whoever does not thank people (for their favours) has not thanked Allah (properly), Mighty and Glorious is He'! (*Ahmad, Tirmidhi*)

140

قَالَ رَسُولُ اللّٰهِ صَلَّى اللّٰهُ عَلَيْهِ وَسَلَّمَ: إِذَا كُنْتُمْ ثَلَاثَةً فَلَا يَتَنَاجَى رَجُلَانِ دُونَ الْآخَرِ حَتَّى تَخْتَلِطُوا بِالنَّاسِ أَجْلَ أَنْ يُحْزِنَهُ. (البخاري ومسلم)

THE PROPHET ﷺ said: 'Whenever there are three of you (in one place), two of you should not talk privately without the third until you are in company of other people, so that his or her feelings will not be hurt'. (*Bukhari, Muslim*)

141

قَالَ رَسُولُ اللّٰهِ صَلَّى اللّٰهُ عَلَيْهِ وَسَلَّمَ: لَا يَحِلُّ لِرَجُلٍ أَنْ يُفَرِّقَ بَيْنَ اثْنَيْنِ إِلَّا بِإِذْنِهِمَا. (أبو داود)

THE PROPHET ﷺ said: 'It is not permitted for anyone to come between two people (sitting or standing) unless he asks their permission'. (*Abu Dawud*)

142

قَالَ رَسُولُ اللّٰهِ صَلَّى اللّٰهُ عَلَيْهِ وَسَلَّمَ: يَسِّرُوا وَلَا تُعَسِّرُوا، وَبَشِّرُوا وَلَا تُنَفِّرُوا. (البخاري ومسلم)

THE PROPHET ﷺ said: 'Make things easy (for people) and do not make them difficult, and cheer people up and do not put them off (by your behaviour)'. (*Bukhari, Muslim*)

Greeting People

143

قَالَ رَسُولُ اللهِ صَلَّى اللهُ عَلَيْهِ وَسَلَّمَ لِأَنَسٍ رَضِيَ اللهُ عَنْهُ: يَا بُنَيَّ إِذَا دَخَلْتَ عَلَى أَهْلِكَ فَسَلِّمْ يَكُنْ بَرَكَةً عَلَيْكَ وَعَلَى أَهْلِ بَيْتِكَ. (الترمذي)

THE PROPHET ﷺ said to Anas ﵁: 'O my dear son, whenever you enter your home greet your family members by saying: as-salāmu ʿalaykum (peace be with you). It will be a blessing for you and the people of your household'. (*Tirmidhi*)

144

قَالَ رَسُولُ اللهِ صَلَّى اللهُ عَلَيْهِ وَسَلَّمَ: يُسَلِّمُ الصَّغِيرُ عَلَى الْكَبِيرِ، وَالْمَارُّ عَلَى الْقَاعِدِ، وَالْقَلِيلُ عَلَى الْكَثِيرِ. (البخاري)

THE PROPHET ﷺ said: 'The younger person should be the first to greet the older one, and the passer-by should greet the one who is sitting or standing, and the small (group) should greet the larger one'. (*Bukhari*)

145

سَأَلَ رَجُلٌ النَّبِيَّ صَلَّى اللَّهُ عَلَيْهِ وَسَلَّمَ: أَيُّ الْإِسْلَامِ خَيْرٌ؟ قَالَ: تُطْعِمُ الطَّعَامَ، وَتَقْرَأُ السَّلَامَ عَلَى مَنْ عَرَفْتَ وَ مَنْ لَمْ تَعْرِفْ. (البخاري)

A MAN once asked the Prophet ﷺ: 'What is the best thing in Islam?' He replied, 'To feed people, and greet both those you know and those you do not know (with as-salāmu ʿalaykum)'. (*Bukhari*)

146

عَنِ الْبَرَاءِ بْنِ عَازِبٍ رَضِيَ اللَّهُ عَنْهُ قَالَ: أَمَرَنَا النَّبِيُّ صَلَّى اللَّهُ عَلَيْهِ وَسَلَّمَ بِسَبْعٍ وَنَهَانَا عَنْ سَبْعٍ، فَذَكَرَ عِيَادَةَ الْمَرِيضِ، وَاتِّبَاعَ الْجَنَائِزِ، وَتَشْمِيتَ الْعَاطِسِ، وَرَدَّ السَّلَامِ، وَنَصْرَ الْمَظْلُومِ، وَإِجَابَةَ الدَّاعِي، وَإِبْرَارَ الْمُقْسِمِ. (البخاري ومسلم)

AL BARA' ibn ʿAzib ﷺ relates: 'The Prophet ﷺ asked us to do seven things: to visit the sick, to follow funeral processions, to pray for Allah's mercy for someone who sneezes (by saying yarhamukallah), to return greetings, help those who are wronged, accept invitations, and fulfil our oaths and promises'. (*Bukhari, Muslim*)

Health and Hygiene

147

عَنْ عَبْدَ اللهِ بْنَ عَمْرٍو رَضِيَ اللهُ عَنْهُمَا قال: قَالَ لِي النَّبِيُّ صَلَّى اللهُ عَلَيْهِ وَسَلَّمَ: أَلَمْ أُخْبَرْ
أَنَّكَ تَقُومُ اللَّيْلَ، وَتَصُومُ النَّهَارَ؟ قُلْتُ: إِنِّي أَفْعَلُ ذَلِكَ، قَالَ: فَإِنَّكَ إِذَا فَعَلْتَ ذَلِكَ هَجَمَتْ
عَيْنُكَ، وَنَفِهَتْ نَفْسُكَ، وَإِنَّ لِنَفْسِكَ حَقًّا، وَلِأَهْلِكَ حَقًّا، فَصُمْ وَأَفْطِرْ، وَقُمْ وَنَمْ. (البخاري)

'ABDULLAH ibn 'Amr ﷺ said: 'The Prophet ﷺ told me: "I have been informed that you stay up all night and fast all day". I replied, "Yes, that is what I do". The Prophet ﷺ said: "But if you do that, you will strain your eyes and your body will be weakened. Your (body and) soul have a right (to rest) over you, and your family has a right over you – So fast but also break your fast, and stand (in prayer at night) but also sleep"'. (*Bukhari*)

148

قَالَ رَسُولَ اللهِ صَلَّى اللهُ عَلَيْهِ وَسَلَّمَ: الطُّهُورُ شَطْرُ الْإِيمَانِ. (مسلم)

THE PROPHET ﷺ said: 'Purity (or cleanliness) is half of faith'.[4] (*Muslim*)

---

4.   This refers to purity of body, mind and soul.

149

قَالَ رَسُولُ اللَّهِ صَلَّى اللَّهُ عَلَيْهِ وَسَلَّمَ: حَقٌّ لِلَّهِ عَلَى كُلِّ مُسْلِمٍ أَنْ يَغْتَسِلَ فِي كُلِّ سَبْعَةِ أَيَّامٍ، يَغْسِلُ رَأْسَهُ وَجَسَدَهُ. (مسلم)

THE PROPHET ﷺ said: 'A right that Allah has over every Muslim is that he bathe himself (at least once) every seven days, washing his head and his body'. (*Muslim*)

150

أَتَى رَسُولُ اللَّهِ صَلَّى اللهُ عَلَيْهِ وَسَلَّمَ فَرَأَى رَجُلًا شَعِثًا قَدْ تَفَرَّقَ شَعْرُهُ، فَقَالَ: أَمَا كَانَ يَجِدُ هَذَا مَا يُسْكِنُ بِهِ شَعْرَهُ؟ وَرَأَى رَجُلًا آخَرَ وَعَلَيْهِ ثِيَابٌ وَسِخَةٌ فَقَالَ: أَمَا كَانَ هَذَا يَجِدُ مَاءً يَغْسِلُ بِهِ ثَوْبَهُ. (أحمد والنسائي)

THE PROPHET ﷺ saw a man whose hair was untidy, and said: 'Couldn't this man find something to comb his hair with?' And he saw a man with dirty clothes and said, 'Couldn't this man find something to wash his clothes with'? (*Ahmad, Nasa'i*)

151

قَالَ رَسُولُ اللَّهِ صَلَّى اللَّهُ عَلَيْهِ وَسَلَّمَ: السِّوَاكُ مَطْهَرَةٌ لِلْفَمِ، مَرْضَاةٌ لِلرَّبِّ. (النسائي)

THE PROPHET ﷺ said: 'Brushing the teeth purifies the mouth and is pleasing to the Lord'. (*Nasa'i*)

152

قَالَ رَسُولُ اللَّهِ صَلَّى اللَّهُ عَلَيْهِ وَسَلَّمَ: لَوْلَا أَنْ أَشُقَّ عَلَى أُمَّتِي أَوْ عَلَى النَّاسِ، لَأَمَرْتُهُمْ بِالسِّوَاكِ مَعَ كُلِّ صَلَاةٍ. (البخاري ومسلم)

THE PROPHET ﷺ said: 'If it were not that I would be putting people to hardship, I would have ordered them to brush their teeth before every Prayer'. (*Bukhari, Muslim*)

153

قَالَ رَسُولُ اللَّهِ صَلَّى اللَّهُ عَلَيْهِ وَسَلَّمَ: نِعْمَتَانِ مَغْبُونٌ فِيهِمَا كَثِيرٌ مِنَ النَّاسِ، الصِّحَّةُ وَالْفَرَاغُ. (البخاري)

THE PROPHET ﷺ said: 'There are two blessings that many people fail to make the most of: good health and free time'. (*Bukhari*)

Table Manners

154

قَالَ رَسُولُ اللَّهِ صَلَّى اللَّهُ عَلَيْهِ وَسَلَّمَ: كُلُوا جَمِيعًا وَلَا تَفَرَّقُوا، فَإِنَّ الْبَرَكَةَ مَعَ الْجَمَاعَةِ. (ابن ماجه)

THE PROPHET ﷺ said: 'Eat together and do not separate, for the blessing is in companionship'. (*Ibn Majah*)

155

قَالَ رَسُولُ اللَّهِ صَلَّى اللَّهُ عَلَيْهِ وَسَلَّمَ: يَا غُلَامُ سَمِّ اللَّهَ، وَكُلْ بِيَمِينِكَ، وَكُلْ مِمَّا يَلِيكَ.
(البخاري ومسلم)

THE PROPHET ﷺ said: 'Young man, mention Allah's name (by saying Bismillah at the beginning of a meal), eat with your right hand, and take what is nearest to you (on the platter)'. (*Bukhari, Muslim*)

156

عَنْ أَبِي هُرَيْرَةَ رَضِيَ اللَّهُ عَنْهُ قَالَ: مَا عَابَ رَسُولُ اللَّهِ صَلَّى اللَّهُ عَلَيْهِ وَسَلَّمَ طَعَامًا قَطُّ، كَانَ إِذَا اشْتَهَى شَيْئًا أَكَلَهُ، وَإِنْ كَرِهَهُ تَرَكَهُ. (مسلم)

ABU HURAYRAH ﷺ said: 'Allah's Messenger ﷺ never complained about food. If he liked something he ate it, and if he didn't like it he left it alone'. (*Muslim*)

157

قَالَ رَسُولُ اللَّهِ صَلَّى اللَّهُ عَلَيْهِ وَسَلَّمَ: طَعَامُ الِاثْنَيْنِ كَافٍ لِثَلَاثَةٍ، وَطَعَامُ الثَّلَاثَةِ كَافٍ لِأَرْبَعَةٍ.
(البخاري ومسلم)

THE PROPHET ﷺ said: 'The food of two people is enough for three, and the food of three people is enough for four'. (*Bukhari, Muslim*)

158

قَالَ رَسُولُ اللّٰهِ صَلَّى اللّٰهُ عَلَيْهِ وَسَلَّمَ: مَا مَلَأَ آدَمِيٌّ وِعَاءً شَرًّا مِنْ بَطْنِهِ، بِحَسْبِ ابْنِ آدَمَ أُكُلَاتٌ

يُقِمْنَ صُلْبَهُ، فَإِنْ كَانَ لَا مَحَالَةَ فَثُلُثٌ لِطَعَامِهِ، وَثُلُثٌ لِشَرَابِهِ، وَثُلُثٌ لِنَفَسِهِ. (الترمذي)

THE PROPHET said: 'There is no worse container for a human being to fill than his belly. It should be enough for a son of Adam to eat just enough food to keep his back straight; but if need be, let him fill one-third (of his stomach) with food and another third with drink, and leave one-third empty for easy breathing'. (*Tirmidhi*)

159

كَانَ النَّبِيُّ صَلَّى اللّٰهُ عَلَيْهِ وَسَلَّمَ إِذَا فَرَغَ مِنْ طَعَامِهِ قَالَ: الْحَمْدُ لِلّٰهِ الَّذِي أَطْعَمَنَا وَسَقَانَا وَجَعَلَنَا

مُسْلِمِينَ. (أبو داود والترمذي)

THE PROPHET used to say at the end of his meal: 'Praise be to Allah, Who gave us food and drink and made us Muslims'. (*Abu Dawud, Tirmidhi*)

Modesty

160

قَالَ رَسُولُ اللّٰهِ صَلَّى اللّٰهُ عَلَيْهِ وَسَلَّمَ: الْحَيَاءُ مِنْ الْإِيمَانِ. (مسلم)

THE PROPHET said: 'Modesty is part of faith'. (*Muslim*)

161

قَالَ رَسُولُ اللَّهِ صَلَّى اللَّهُ عَلَيْهِ وَسَلَّمَ: إِنَّ لِكُلِّ دِينٍ خُلُقًا، وَخُلُقُ الْإِسْلَامِ الْحَيَاءُ.
(ابن ماجه ومالك)

THE PROPHET ﷺ said: 'Every religion has a distinctive characteristic, and the characteristic of Islam is modesty'. (*Ibn Majah, Malik*)

Patience

162

قَالَ رَسُولُ اللَّهِ صَلَّى اللَّهُ عَلَيْهِ وَسَلَّمَ: عَجَبًا لِأَمْرِ الْمُؤْمِنِ، إِنَّ أَمْرَهُ كُلَّهُ خَيْرٌ وَلَيْسَ ذَاكَ لِأَحَدٍ
إِلَّا لِلْمُؤْمِنِ، إِنْ أَصَابَتْهُ سَرَّاءُ شَكَرَ فَكَانَ خَيْرًا لَهُ، وَإِنْ أَصَابَتْهُ ضَرَّاءُ صَبَرَ فَكَانَ خَيْرًا لَهُ. (مسلم)

THE PROPHET ﷺ said: 'How wonderful the situation of a believer is: Everything is good for him, and this is only true for a believer. For if he encounters good, he is grateful to Allah and that is good for him; and if he is afflicted with hardship, he is patient and that is good for him'. (*Muslim*)

163

قَالَ رَسُولُ اللَّهِ صَلَّى اللَّهُ عَلَيْهِ وَسَلَّمَ: مَا يُصِيبُ الْمُسْلِمَ مِنْ نَصَبٍ وَلَا وَصَبٍ، وَلَا هَمٍّ وَلَا حُزْنٍ، وَلَا أَذًى وَلَا غَمٍّ، حَتَّى الشَّوْكَةَ يُشَاكُهَا إِلَّا كَفَّرَ اللَّهُ بِهَا مِنْ خَطَايَاهُ. (البخاري ومسلم)

THE PROPHET ﷺ said: 'Whenever a Muslim is afflicted by any hardship – whether a stress, an illness, worry, grief, harm, disturbance, or even the prick of a thorn – Allah removes some of the wrong actions (from his record) because of it'. (*Bukhari, Muslim*)

164

قَالَ رَسُولُ اللَّهِ صَلَّى اللَّهُ عَلَيْهِ وَسَلَّمَ: إِنَّ عِظَمَ الْجَزَاءِ مَعَ عِظَمِ الْبَلَاءِ، وَإِنَّ الله إِذَا أَحَبَّ قَوْماً ابْتَلَاهُمْ، فَمَنْ رَضِيَ فَلَهُ الرِّضَا، وَمَنْ سَخِطَ فَلَهُ السَّخَطُ (الترمذي وابن ماجه)

THE PROPHET ﷺ said: 'Great rewards are given for great trials, and when Allah loves a people, He tests them. Whoever accepts the trial cheerfully earns His good pleasure, and whoever resents it earns His wrath'. (*Tirmidhi, Ibn Majah*)

Honesty and Trustworthiness

165

قَالَ رَسُولُ اللَّهِ صَلَّى اللَّهُ عَلَيْهِ وَسَلَّمَ: إِنَّ الصِّدْقَ يَهْدِي إِلَى الْبِرِّ، وَإِنَّ الْبِرَّ يَهْدِي إِلَى الْجَنَّةِ، وَإِنَّ الرَّجُلَ لَيَصْدُقُ حَتَّى يُكْتَبَ عِنْدَ اللَّهِ صِدِّيقًا، وَإِنَّ الْكَذِبَ يَهْدِي إِلَى الْفُجُورِ، وَإِنَّ الْفُجُورَ يَهْدِي إِلَى النَّارِ، وَإِنَّ الرَّجُلَ لَيَكْذِبُ حَتَّى يُكْتَبَ عِنْدَ اللَّهِ كَذَّابًا. (البخاري ومسلم)

THE PROPHET ﷺ said: '(Always tell the truth) for the truth will guide you to goodness, and goodness leads to Paradise. A man continues to tell the truth until he is recorded with Allah as a man of truth. Avoid lying, for lying leads to immorality, and immorality leads to Hell. A man continues to tell lies until he is written down with Allah as being a habitual liar'. (*Bukhari, Muslim*)

166

قَالَ رَسُولَ اللَّهِ صَلَّى اللَّهُ عَلَيْهِ وَسَلَّمَ: وَيْلٌ لِلَّذِي يُحَدِّثُ فَيَكْذِبُ لِيُضْحِكَ بِهِ الْقَوْمَ، وَيْلٌ لَهُ، وَيْلٌ لَهُ. (أبو داود والترمذي)

THE PROPHET ﷺ said: 'Shame on the one who tells lies in order to make people laugh! Shame on him! Shame on him'! (*Abu Dawud, Tirmidhi*)

167

قَالَ رَسُولُ اللَّهِ صَلَّى اللَّهُ عَلَيْهِ وَسَلَّمَ: كَفَى بِالْمَرْءِ كَذِبًا أَنْ يُحَدِّثَ بِكُلِّ مَا سَمِعَ. (مسلم)

THE PROPHET ﷺ said: 'It is enough to make a person a liar that he should repeat everything he hears'. (*Muslim*)

168

قَالَ رَسُولُ اللَّهِ صَلَّى اللَّهُ عَلَيْهِ وَسَلَّمَ: لَا إِيمَانَ لِمَنْ لَا أَمَانَةَ لَهُ، وَلَا دِينَ لِمَنْ لَا عَهْدَ لَهُ. (البيهقي)

THE PROPHET ﷺ said: 'He who is not trustworthy has no faith, and he who does not keep his word has no religion'. (*Bayhaqi*)

169

قَالَ رَسُولُ اللَّهِ صَلَّى اللَّهُ عَلَيْهِ وَسَلَّمَ: عَلَامَاتُ الْمُنَافِقِ ثَلَاثٌ، إِذَا حَدَّثَ كَذَبَ، وَإِذَا وَعَدَ أَخْلَفَ، وَإِذَا اؤْتُمِنَ خَانَ. وَفِي رِوَايَةِ مسلم وَإِنْ صَامَ وَصَلَّى وَزَعَمَ أَنَّهُ مُسْلِمٌ. (البخاري ومسلم)

THE PROPHET ﷺ said: 'Three signs of a hypocrite are: when he talks, he lies; When he makes a promise, he breaks it; and when he is entrusted with something, he betrays his trust. [Muslim's version adds:] Even if he joins in the prayer, observes the fast, and claims to be a Muslim'. (*Bukhari, Muslim*)

Forgiveness

170

حَكَى رَسُولُ اللَّهِ صَلَّى اللَّهُ عَلَيْهِ وَسَلَّمَ: عَنْ نَبِيٍّ مِنَ الْأَنْبِيَاءِ ضَرَبَهُ قَوْمُهُ فَأَدْمَوْهُ وَهُوَ يَمْسَحُ الدَّمَ عَنْ وَجْهِهِ وَيَقُولُ: اللَّهُمَّ اغْفِرْ لِقَوْمِي فَإِنَّهُمْ لَا يَعْلَمُونَ. (البخاري)

THE PROPHET ﷺ once spoke about one of the Prophets, whose people had beaten him and caused him to bleed, and while he was wiping the blood from his face he said: 'O Allah, forgive my people, for they do not understand (what they are doing)'. (*Bukhari*)

171

قَالَ رَسُولُ اللَّهِ صَلَّى اللَّهُ عَلَيْهِ وَسَلَّمَ: مَا مِنْ رَجُلٍ يُصَابُ بِشَيْءٍ فِي جَسَدِهِ فَيَتَصَدَّقُ بِهِ، إِلاَّ رَفَعَهُ اللهُ بِهِ دَرَجَةً وَحَطَّ عَنْهُ بِهِ خَطِيئَةً. (الترمذي)

THE PROPHET ﷺ said: 'Whoever suffers an injury done to him and forgives (the person responsible), Allah will raise his status to a higher degree and remove one of his sins'. (*Tirmidhi*)

Minding one's own business

172

قَالَ رَسُولُ اللَّهِ صَلَّى اللَّهُ عَلَيْهِ وَسَلَّمَ: ...لَا تَجَسَّسُوا... (البخاري)

THE PROPHET ﷺ said: 'Do not spy on one another'. (*Bukhari*)

173

قَالَ رَسُولُ اللَّهِ صَلَّى اللَّهُ عَلَيْهِ وَسَلَّمَ: مِنْ حُسْنِ إِسْلَامِ الْمَرْءِ تَرْكُهُ مَا لَا يَعْنِيهِ. (الترمذي)

THE PROPHET ﷺ said: 'Part of being a good Muslim is to leave alone whatever does not concern him'. (*Tirmidhi*)

Contentment

174

قَالَ رَسُولُ اللَّهِ صَلَّى اللَّهُ عَلَيْهِ وَسَلَّمَ: انْظُرُوا إِلَى مَنْ أَسْفَلَ مِنْكُمْ وَلَا تَنْظُرُوا إِلَى مَنْ هُوَ فَوْقَكُمْ فَهُوَ أَجْدَرُ أَنْ لَا تَزْدَرُوا نِعْمَةَ اللَّهِ عَلَيْكُمْ. (مسلم)

THE PROPHET ﷺ said: 'Look at those who are worse off than you; do not look at those who are above you (in wealth, looks, or other things), for then you will not be ungrateful for the blessings that Allah has given you'. (*Muslim*)

175

قَالَ رَسُولُ اللَّهِ صَلَّى اللَّهُ عَلَيْهِ وَسَلَّمَ: لَيْسَ الْغِنَى عَنْ كَثْرَةِ الْعَرْضِ وَلَكِنَّ الْغِنَى غِنَى النَّفْسِ.
(البخاري ومسلم)

THE PROPHET ﷺ said: 'Wealth does not come from having great riches; (true) wealth is contentment of the soul'. (*Bukhari, Muslim*)

176

عَنْ سَهْلِ بْنِ سَعْدٍ السَّاعِدِيِّ رَضِيَّ الله عَنْهُ قَالَ: أَتَى النَّبِيَّ صَلَّى الله عَلَيْهِ وَسَلَّمَ رَجُلٌ فَقَالَ يَا رَسُولَ الله دُلَّنِي عَلَى عَمَلٍ إِذَا أَنَا عَمِلْتُهُ أَحَبَّنِيَّ الله وَأَحَبَّنِيَّ النَّاسُ، فَقَالَ رَسُولُ الله صَلَّى الله عَلَيْهِ وَسَلَّمَ: ازْهَدْ فِي الدُّنْيَا يُحِبُّكَ الله وَازْهَدْ فِيمَا فِي أَيْدِي النَّاسِ يُحِبُّوكَ. (ابن ماجه)

SAHL ibn Sa'd al-Sa'idi ﷺ said: 'A man came to the Prophet ﷺ and asked him: "Please tell me of something that I can do so that both Allah as well as people will love me". The Prophet ﷺ said: "Do not be attached to this world and Allah will love you and do not go after other people's possessions (desire what is in other people's hands) and they will love you'. (*Ibn Majah*)

28

Things to Guard Against

وَلَا تُصَعِّرْ خَدَّكَ لِلنَّاسِ وَلَا تَمْشِ فِى ٱلْأَرْضِ مَرَحًا إِنَّ ٱللَّهَ لَا يُحِبُّ كُلَّ مُخْتَالٍ فَخُورٍ ۝

وَٱقْصِدْ فِى مَشْيِكَ وَٱغْضُضْ مِن صَوْتِكَ إِنَّ أَنكَرَ ٱلْأَصْوَٰتِ لَصَوْتُ ٱلْحَمِيرِ ۝

(Luqman advised his son): Do not turn your face away from people with pride, or walk arrogantly through the earth. Surely Allah does not like any arrogant show-off. Be moderate in your gait, and lower your voice. Truly, the harshest of all voices is the braying of the donkey. (al-Qur'an 31: 18-19)

Major Sins

✳

1̸7̸7̸

سُئِلَ النَّبِيُّ صَلَّى اللَّهُ عَلَيْهِ وَسَلَّمَ عَنِ الْكَبَائِرِ فَقَالَ: الْإِشْرَاكُ بِاللَّهِ، وَعُقُوقُ الْوَالِدَيْنِ، وَقَتْلُ النَّفْسِ، وَشَهَادَةُ الزُّورِ. (البخاري)

THE PROPHET ﷺ was asked about the major sins, and he mentioned: 'To worship other gods besides Allah (the One God), to disobey your parents, to commit murder and to give false testimony'. (*Bukhari*)

Pride and Arrogance

✳

1̸7̸8̸

قَالَ رَسُولُ اللَّهِ صَلَّى اللَّهُ عَلَيْهِ وَسَلَّمَ: لَا يَدْخُلُ الْجَنَّةَ مَنْ كَانَ فِي قَلْبِهِ مِثْقَالُ ذَرَّةٍ مِنْ كِبْرٍ، قَالَ رَجُلٌ إِنَّ الرَّجُلَ يُحِبُّ أَنْ يَكُونَ ثَوْبُهُ حَسَنًا وَنَعْلُهُ حَسَنَةً، قَالَ إِنَّ اللَّهَ جَمِيلٌ يُحِبُّ الْجَمَالَ، الْكِبْرُ بَطَرُ الْحَقِّ وَغَمْطُ النَّاسِ. (مسلم)

THE PROPHET ﷺ said: 'Whoever has pride in his heart equal to the weight of a mustard seed shall not enter Paradise.' Someone said, 'A person likes to wear beautiful clothes and fine shoes.' He replied, 'Allah is beautiful and likes beauty. Pride means rejecting the truth and looking down on other people'. (*Muslim*)

✳

179

قَالَ رَسُولَ اللَّهِ صَلَّى اللَّهُ عَلَيْهِ وَسَلَّمَ: كُلُوا وَاشْرَبُوا وَتَصَدَّقُوا وَالْبِسُوا فِي غَيْرِ مَخِيلَةٍ وَلَا سَرَفٍ،

إِنَّ اللَّهَ يُحِبُّ أَنْ تُرَى نِعْمَتُهُ عَلَى عَبْدِهِ. (أحمد وابن ماجه)

THE PROPHET ﷺ said: 'Eat, drink, give charity and wear (nice) clothes, (as long as you do so) without arrogance or extravagance. Allah loves that His blessings be seen on His servant'. (*Ahmad, Ibn Majah*)

✳

180

قَالَ رَسُولَ اللَّهِ صَلَّى اللَّهُ عَلَيْهِ وَسَلَّمَ: إِنَّ اللَّهَ عَزَّ وَجَلَّ قَدْ أَذْهَبَ عَنْكُمْ عُبِّيَّةَ الْجَاهِلِيَّةِ وَفَخْرَهَا

بِالْآبَاءِ، مُؤْمِنٌ تَقِيٌّ، وَفَاجِرٌ شَقِيٌّ، وَالنَّاسُ بَنُو آدَمَ، وَآدَمُ مِنْ تُرَابٍ. (أحمد وأبو داود)

THE PROPHET ﷺ said: 'Indeed, Allah has saved you from the ignorant practices (of the days before Islam) and the bad habits of boasting about ancestors. A person is only a pious believer or a miserable sinner. All people are the children of Adam, and Adam was created from dust'. (*Ahmad, Abu Dawud*)

✳

181

قَالَ رَسُولُ اللَّهِ صَلَّى اللَّهُ عَلَيْهِ وَسَلَّمَ: أَلَا أَدُلُّكُمْ عَلَى ... أَهْلِ النَّارِ، كُلُّ جَوَّاظٍ عُتُلٍّ مُسْتَكْبِرٍ.

(البخاري)

THE PROPHET ﷺ said: 'Shall I not tell you who the inhabitants of Hell are? They are the people who are stuck-up, arrogant and stubborn'. (*Bukhari*)

Anger

❋

182

عَنْ أَبِي هُرَيْرَةَ رَضِيَ اللَّهُ عَنْهُ أَنَّ رَجُلًا قَالَ لِلنَّبِيِّ صَلَّى اللَّهُ عَلَيْهِ وَسَلَّمَ: أَوْصِنِي قَالَ لَا تَغْضَبْ، لَا تَغْضَبْ، لَا تَغْضَبْ. (البخاري، والترمذي، وأحمد)

ABU HURAYRAH ﷺ related that a man came to the Prophet ﷺ and said: 'Please give me some advice'. The Prophet ﷺ said: 'Do not become angry (i.e. do not lose your temper), do not become angry, do not become angry'. (*Bukhari, Tirmidhi, Ahmad*)

❋

183

قَالَ رَسُولُ اللَّهِ صَلَّى اللَّهُ عَلَيْهِ وَسَلَّمَ: لَيْسَ الشَّدِيدُ بِالصُّرَعَةِ، إِنَّمَا الشَّدِيدُ الَّذِي يَمْلِكُ نَفْسَهُ عِنْدَ الْغَضَبِ. (البخاري، ومسلم، وأحمد، ومالك)

THE PROPHET ﷺ said: 'The strong man is not the one who knocks others down, but the one who controls himself when angry'. (*Bukhari, Muslim, Ahmad, Malik*)

✳

184

قَالَ رَسُولُ اللَّهِ صَلَّى اللَّهُ عَلَيْهِ وَسَلَّمَ: إِنَّ الْغَضَبَ مِنَ الشَّيْطَانِ وَإِنَّ الشَّيْطَانَ خُلِقَ مِنَ النَّارِ

وَإِنَّمَا تُطْفَأُ النَّارُ بِالْمَاءِ فَإِذَا غَضِبَ أَحَدُكُمْ فَلْيَتَوَضَّأْ (أبو داود وأحمد)

THE PROPHET ﷺ said: 'Anger comes from Satan, and Satan was created from fire. It is water that extinguishes fire, so if any of you becomes angry he should make ablution'. (*Abu Dawud, Ahmad*)

Jealousy, Envy and Hatred

✳

185

قَالَ رَسُولُ اللَّهِ صَلَّى اللَّهُ عَلَيْهِ وَسَلَّمَ: إِيَّاكُمْ وَالْحَسَدَ فَإِنَّ الْحَسَدَ يَأْكُلُ الْحَسَنَاتِ كَمَا تَأْكُلُ

النَّارُ الْحَطَبَ (أبو داود)

THE PROPHET ﷺ said: 'Beware of envy, for envy destroys good deeds the way fire consumes firewood'. (*Abu Dawud*)

✳

186

قَالَ رَسُولُ اللَّهِ صَلَّى اللَّهُ عَلَيْهِ وَسَلَّمَ: لَا حَسَدَ إِلَّا فِي اثْنَتَيْنِ رَجُلٌ آتَاهُ اللَّهُ مَالًا فَسُلِّطَ عَلَى هَلَكَتِهِ

فِي الْحَقِّ وَرَجُلٌ آتَاهُ اللَّهُ الْحِكْمَةَ فَهُوَ يَقْضِي بِهَا وَيُعَلِّمُهَا. (البخاري)

THE PROPHET ﷺ said: 'There are only two (kinds of) people worth envying: someone whom Allah has made rich, and who spends his money righteously; and someone whom Allah has given wisdom (the Holy Qur'an), and who acts according to it, and teaches it'. (*Bukhari*)

❋

187

قَالَ أَنَسُ بْنُ مَالِكٍ قَالَ لِي رَسُولُ اللّٰهِ صَلَّى اللّٰهُ عَلَيْهِ وَسَلَّمَ يَا بُنَيَّ إِنْ قَدَرْتَ أَنْ تُصْبِحَ وَتُمْسِيَ، لَيْسَ فِي قَلْبِكَ غِشٌّ لِأَحَدٍ فَافْعَلْ. (الترمذي)

ANAS ibn Malik ﷺ relates: 'Allah's Messenger ﷺ said to me, "O my son, if you can spend each morning and evening with a heart free of hatred or deception against anyone, then do so"'. (*Tirmidhi*)

Hypocrisy

❋

188

عَنْ مُحَمَّدِ بْنِ زَيْدِ بْنِ عَبْدِ اللّٰهِ بْنِ عُمَرَ عَنْ أَبِيهِ قَالَ أُنَاسٌ لِابْنِ عُمَرَ إِنَّا نَدْخُلُ عَلَى سُلْطَانِنَا، فَنَقُولُ لَهُمْ خِلَافَ مَا نَتَكَلَّمُ بِهِ إِذَا خَرَجْنَا مِنْ عِنْدِهِمْ قَالَ كُنَّا نَعُدُّهَا نِفَاقاً (البخاري)

MUHAMMAD ibn Zayd ﷺ relates that some people confessed to his grandfather Abdullah ibn ʿUmar: 'When we go to our rulers, we say things to them that are different from what we say when we leave them.' Abdullah son of ʿUmar told them, 'We used to consider this to be hypocrisy'. (*Bukhari*)

189

قَالَ رَسُولَ اللهِ صَلَّى اللهُ عَلَيْهِ وَسَلَّمَ: مَنْ كَانَ ذَا وَجْهَيْنِ فِي الدُّنْيَا، كَانَ لَهُ لِسَانَانِ

مِنْ نَّارٍ يَوْمَ الْقِيَامَةِ. (أبو داود)

THE PROPHET ﷺ said: 'Whoever is two-faced (hypocritical) in this world will have two tongues of fire on the Day of Resurrection'. (*Abu Dawud*)

Miserliness and Greed

190

قَالَ رَسُولُ اللهِ صَلَّى اللهُ عَلَيْهِ وَسَلَّمَ: مَا مِنْ يَوْمٍ يُصْبِحُ الْعِبَادُ فِيهِ إِلَّا مَلَكَانِ يَنْزِلَانِ، فَيَقُولُ

أَحَدُهُمَا اللَّهُمَّ أَعْطِ مُنْفِقًا خَلَفًا، وَيَقُولُ الْآخَرُ اللَّهُمَّ أَعْطِ مُمْسِكًا تَلَفًا (البخاري)

THE PROPHET ﷺ said: 'Every morning at dawn, two angels descend and one of them says, 'O Allah, give more to the person who spends in charity!' while the other one says, 'O Allah, destroy the wealth of the miser'! (*Bukhari*)

Guarding one's tongue

✳

191

قَالَ رَسُولُ اللَّهِ صَلَّى اللَّهُ عَلَيْهِ وَسَلَّمَ: مَنْ كَانَ يُؤْمِنُ بِاللَّهِ وَالْيَوْمِ الْآخِرِ فَلْيَقُلْ خَيْرًا أَوْ لِيَصْمُتْ. (البخاري ومسلم)

THE PROPHET ﷺ said: 'Whoever believes in Allah and the Last Day should say what is good, or be silent'. (*Bukhari, Muslim*)

✳

192

قَالَ رَسُولُ اللَّهِ صَلَّى اللَّهُ عَلَيْهِ وَسَلَّمَ: لِأَصْحَابِه: أَتَدْرُونَ مَا الْغِيبَةُ؟ قَالُوا اللَّهُ وَرَسُولُهُ أَعْلَمُ. قَالَ ذِكْرُكَ أَخَاكَ بِمَا يَكْرَهُ، قِيلَ أَفَرَأَيْتَ إِنْ كَانَ فِي أَخِي مَا أَقُولُ، قَالَ إِنْ كَانَ فِيهِ مَا تَقُولُ فَقَدِ اغْتَبْتَهُ، وَإِنْ لَمْ يَكُنْ فِيهِ فَقَدْ بَهَتَّهُ. (مسلم)

THE PROPHET ﷺ said to his Companions: 'Do you know what backbiting is? 'Allah and His Messenger know best,' they replied. 'Backbiting is to say anything about your brother (behind his back) that he would not like,' he explained. Someone asked, 'But what if he is as I say?' The Prophet ﷺ replied, 'If he is as you say, then you are guilty of backbiting, and if he is not, you are guilty of slander'. (*Muslim*)

❋

193

قَالَ رَسُولُ اللَّهِ صَلَّى اللَّهُ عَلَيْهِ وَسَلَّمَ: إِنَّ الْمُؤْمِنَ لَيْسَ بِاللَّعَّانِ وَلَا الطَّعَّانِ وَلَا الْفَاحِشِ وَلَا الْبَذِيءِ. (الترمذي)

THE PROPHET ﷺ said: 'A believer is not a habitual curser, insulter, or one who is in the habit of using foul or obscene language'. (*Tirmidhi*)

❋

194

قَالَ رَسُولُ اللَّهِ صَلَّى اللَّهُ عَلَيْهِ وَسَلَّمَ: هَلَكَ الْمُتَنَطِّعُونَ، هَلَكَ الْمُتَنَطِّعُونَ، هَلَكَ الْمُتَنَطِّعُونَ (مسلم وأبو داود)

THE PROPHET ﷺ said: 'Those who exaggerate will be ruined; those who exaggerate will be ruined; those who exaggerate will be ruined'. (*Muslim, Abu Dawud*)

❋

195

قَالَ رَسُولُ اللَّهِ صَلَّى اللَّهُ عَلَيْهِ وَسَلَّمَ: إِنَّ اللَّهَ يَكْرَهُ لَكُمْ قِيلَ وَقَالَ، وَكَثْرَةَ السُّؤَالِ، وَإِضَاعَةِ الْمَالِ. (مسلم)

THE PROPHET ﷺ said: 'Allah is displeased by your meaningless chatter, your asking too many questions, and wasting money'. (*Muslim*)

29

Some Prayers of the Prophet ﷺ

قُلْ إِن كُنتُمْ تُحِبُّونَ ٱللَّهَ فَٱتَّبِعُونِي يُحْبِبْكُمُ ٱللَّهُ
وَيَغْفِرْ لَكُمْ ذُنُوبَكُمْ وَٱللَّهُ غَفُورٌ رَّحِيمٌ ﴿٣١﴾

Say (to the people, O Muhammad): 'If you love Allah, follow me.
Allah will love you and forgive you your sins.
Allah is Most Forgiving, Most Merciful.' (al-Qur'an 3:31)

196

قَالَ رَسُولُ اللَّهِ صَلَّى اللَّهُ عَلَيْهِ وَسَلَّمَ: اللَّهُمَّ إِنِّي أَعُوذُ بِكَ مِنْ عِلْمٍ لَا يَنْفَعُ، وَمِنْ قَلْبٍ لَا يَخْشَعُ، وَمِنْ نَفْسٍ لَا تَشْبَعُ، وَمِنْ دُعَاءٍ لَا يُسْمَعُ. (الترمذي، والنسائي)

THE PROPHET ﷺ said: 'O Allah, I seek refuge in You from knowledge that does not benefit, a heart that is not submissive, a soul that is dissatisfied, and a prayer that is not heard'. (*Tirmidhi, Nasa'i*)

197

قَالَ رَسُولُ اللَّهِ صَلَّى اللَّهُ عَلَيْهِ وَسَلَّمَ: اللَّهُمَّ إِنِّي أَسْأَلُكَ فِعْلَ الْخَيْرَاتِ، وَتَرْكَ الْمُنْكَرَاتِ، وَحُبَّ الْمَسَاكِينِ، وَأَنْ تَغْفِرَ لِي وَتَرْحَمَنِي، وَإِذَا أَرَدْتَ فِتْنَةً فِي قَوْمٍ فَتَوَفَّنِي غَيْرَ مَفْتُونٍ، وَأَسْأَلُكَ حُبَّكَ، وَحُبَّ مَنْ يُحِبُّكَ، وَحُبَّ عَمَلٍ يُقَرِّبُنِي إِلَى حُبِّكَ. (احمد)

THE PROPHET ﷺ said: 'O Allah, I ask You to make it easy for me to do what is good, to leave what is bad, and to love the needy. And I ask You to forgive me and have mercy on me. If it is Your will that some people be put to severe trials, take my soul without letting me fall into temptation. And I ask You for Your love, and the love of those who love You, and the love of deeds that draw me near to Your love'. (*Ahmad*)

The prayer for making a choice or decision (Istikharah):

198

قَالَ رَسُولُ اللهِ صَلَّى اللهُ عَلَيْهِ وَسَلَّمَ: اللَّهُمَّ إِنِّي أَسْتَخِيرُكَ بِعِلْمِكَ وَأَسْتَقْدِرُكَ بِقُدْرَتِكَ وَأَسْأَلُكَ مِنْ فَضْلِكَ الْعَظِيمِ فَإِنَّكَ تَقْدِرُ وَلَا أَقْدِرُ وَتَعْلَمُ وَلَا أَعْلَمُ وَأَنْتَ عَلَّامُ الْغُيُوبِ. اللَّهُمَّ إِنْ كُنْتَ تَعْلَمُ أَنَّ هَذَا الْأَمْرَ خَيْرٌ لِي فِي دِينِي وَمَعَاشِي وَعَاقِبَةِ أَمْرِي أَوْ قَالَ فِي عَاجِلِ أَمْرِي وَآجِلِهِ فَاقْدُرْهُ لِي وَإِنْ كُنْتَ تَعْلَمُ أَنَّ هَذَا الْأَمْرَ شَرٌّ لِي فِي دِينِي وَمَعَاشِي وَعَاقِبَةِ أَمْرِي أَوْ قَالَ فِي عَاجِلِ أَمْرِي وَآجِلِهِ فَاصْرِفْهُ عَنِّي وَاصْرِفْنِي عَنْهُ وَاقْدُرْ لِي الْخَيْرَ حَيْثُ كَانَ ثُمَّ رَضِّنِي بِهِ. (البخاري)

THE PROPHET ﷺ said: 'O Allah, I ask You to enable me to choose what is best through Your knowledge, and bring it to pass through Your power. I ask You to give to me of Your immense favour, for You are All-Powerful, and I am not; You know and I do not; You are the Knower of the Unseen. O Allah, if You know that this matter is best for me in my religion, livelihood and my final end, then bring it about and make it easy for me. And if You know that this matter is bad for me in my religion, livelihood and my final end, Then keep it away from me, and keep me away from it. And bring about what is best for me, whatever it may be, and make me pleased with it'. (*Bukhari*)

199

قَالَ رَسُولُ اللهِ صَلَّى اللهُ عَلَيْهِ وَسَلَّمَ: يَا مُقَلِّبَ الْقُلُوبِ ثَبِّتْ قَلْبِي عَلَى دِينِكَ. (الترمذي)

THE PROPHET ﷺ said: 'O Changer of hearts, make my heart firm in Your religion'. (*Tirmidhi*)

☙ 200 ☙

قَالَ رَسُولُ اللَّهِ صَلَّى اللَّهُ عَلَيْهِ وَسَلَّمَ: مَثَلُ مَا بَعَثَنِي اللَّهُ بِهِ مِنَ الْهُدَى وَالْعِلْمِ كَمَثَلِ الْغَيْثِ الْكَثِيرِ، أَصَابَ أَرْضًا فَكَانَ مِنْهَا نَقِيَّةٌ قَبِلَتُ الْمَاءَ فَأَنْبَتَتُ الْكَلَأَ وَالْعُشْبَ الْكَثِيرَ، وَكَانَتْ مِنْهَا أَجَادِبُ أَمْسَكَتِ الْمَاءَ فَنَفَعَ اللَّهُ بِهَا النَّاسَ فَشَرِبُوا وَسَقَوْا وَزَرَعُوا، وَأَصَابَتْ مِنْهَا طَائِفَةً أُخْرَى إِنَّمَا هِيَ قِيعَانٌ لَا تُمْسِكُ مَاءً وَلَا تُنْبِتُ كَلَأً، فَذَلِكَ مَثَلُ مَنْ فَقُهَ فِي دِينِ اللَّهِ وَنَفَعَهُ مَا بَعَثَنِي اللَّهُ بِهِ فَعَلِمَ وَعَلَّمَ، وَمَثَلُ مَنْ لَمْ يَرْفَعْ بِذَلِكَ رَأْسًا وَلَمْ يَقْبَلْ هُدَى اللَّهِ الَّذِي أُرْسِلْتُ بِهِ. (البخاري)

THE PROPHET ﷺ said: 'The guidance and knowledge that I have been sent with are like abundant rain falling on the earth: Some of the soil was fertile, and it grew plenty of green grass and vegetation. Another portion of it was hard, but it held the rainwater so that Allah made it useful to people: they drank and watered their animals, and used it to irrigate their crops. And a portion of it was barren land that could neither hold the water, nor grow anything. The first (piece of ground) is like those who understand the religion, and benefit from what Allah has sent through me, and learn it, and teach it. (The second is like those who do not understand the knowledge, but pass it on to others so that they benefit from it.) And the last is like the person who does not care for it, and does not accept the guidance I have been sent with. (He is like that barren land)'. (*Bukhari*)

Truly, Allah and His angels send blessings on the Prophet.
O you who believe, ask Allah to bless him,
and salute him with many salutations. (al-Qur'an, 33: 56)